STRIKE

FROM BENEATH THE SEA

A History of Aircraft-carrying Submarines

STRIKE

FROM BENEATH THE SEA

A History of Aircraft-carrying Submarines

Terry C. Treadwell

For my son, Toby

First published 1999
This edition published 2009

The History Press
The Mill, Brimscombe Port
Stroud, Gloucestershire, GL5 2QG
www.thehistorypress.co.uk

© Terry C. Treadwell 1999, 2009

The right of Terry C. Treadwell to be identified as the Author
of this work has been asserted in accordance with the
Copyrights, Designs and Patents Act 1988.

British Library Cataloguing in Publication Data.
A catalogue record for this book is available from the British Library.

ISBN 978 0 7524 5243 2

Typesetting and origination by The History Press
Printed in Great Britain

Contents

Foreword

One day in the late 1940s, when I headed the El Segundo Division of the Douglas Aircraft Company in California, I was contacted by an engineer at the U.S. Office of Naval Research in Washington D.C. He asked if we would be interested in designing a combat aircraft small enough to operate from a submarine.

The idea struck me as a bit crazy at first, but we were in the airplane business and I didn't want to pass up an opportunity for our outstanding design and engineering team to reach out to new horizons. I agreed to look into the matter, briefed my group accordingly, and went to work.

The navy wanted such an airplane in order to attack enemy submarines on the high seas. Carrier-based aircraft were available, but the submarine, as a carrier in miniature, although certainly limited in capability, would provide extra punch. The rocket-powered Regulus missile already existed and functioned well when launched from a submarine. Why not an aircraft with a pilot at the controls?

We designed a small jet-propelled seaplane. Its wings folded flush along the fuselage. This allowed the aircraft to be compactly stored in a cannister mounted on the deck. In order to launch, the submarine had to surface. The airplane would then be extracted and moved aft to a small platform with rails angled steeply skywards.

Once on the rails, the pilot entered the cockpit. Crewmen would unfold the wings, load the weapons onto the machine and start the engine. The plane was so light that JATO – jet assisted take-off – bottles and engine power were sufficient to fire it along the rails into the sky. The submarine would then dive back under the sea while the pilot sought out and attacked the enemy submarine. He would then return to a predetermined recovery point where the sub had surfaced and deployed a platform, like a floating dock, from the stern. The aircraft would land and taxi onto the platform. The aircraft would then be hoisted aboard by a special crane and prepared for the next mission.

Although there were complications in the concept, the design looked good on paper and might have worked. But the submarine-based aircraft never left the drawing board. The US Navy's interest waned and the idea was shelved. We did, however, gain considerable knowledge during the project. Our work with the small dimensions of the plane helped us a few years later when we designed a low-wing monoplane with a reduced aspect ratio. The plane was small compared to other jets that filled the skies of the 1950s and bears a resemblance to its submarine-based predecessor. I refer of course to the light attack bomber, the Douglas A-4 Skyhawk, that came to be known as 'Heinemann's Hot Rod'. Some even called it the 'Tinker Toy'. It flew for the first time in June 1954 and at the time of writing, more than thirty years later, remains in the active military inventory of several countries. I have allowed my friend Terry Treadwell to use the only known photographs on the model known as the Douglas Model 640.

I am pleased that Terry has explored the little known but fascinating history of submarine-aviation. The free-thinking and determined men who tried to mate aircraft with submarines may not have succeeded on a grand scale, but they certainly made important contributions to the world of aeronautics. This book serves as a form of praise for these enterprising engineers, designers, aviators and supporting crews. Well Done!

Ed Heinemann
May 1985

Photograph of the model jet fighter No. NONR-772(00) designed by Ed Heinemann for use on a submarine – starboard side view shot. (USN)

Preface

This re-written edition of *Submarines with Wings*, now retitled *Strike from Beneath the Sea*, first published in 1985, was brought about by the discovery of new information and photographs. The original book started life as an article written for *Naval Aviation News* and, although there have been a number of articles written on the subject of submarine aviation since, it was the first and only book – this is now the second.

The period of submarine aviation only lasted about thirty years, but it never became the success that designers and manufacturers had hoped. But what success they did have proved that submarine-borne aircraft were a viable proposition; one that I believe is still retained in the minds of the military powers today.

Of all the countries to have experimented with submarine-borne aircraft, Japan had the most success militarily, from the Yokosuka 1 in the 1920s to the Yokosuka E14Y1, or 'Glen' as it was known to the Allies, that bombed the West Coast of America in 1942, the first and only time the United States of America was ever bombed. Then there were the Sieran bombers from the giant I-400 Class submarines that so nearly bombed the Gatun Locks at Panama during the Second World War. Japan was the only country to use the submarine-aircraft combination successfully under wartime conditions.

It appears that back in 1914 the Germans first thought of the idea of carrying aircraft on the decks of submarines. They carried a Friedrichshafen FF 29 balanced across the deck of the U-12. The British responded by attempting to launch two Sopwith Schneiders from the deck of the submarine E-22. The British improved on the idea in 1929 by building a hangar on the deck of the M-2 submarine and an aircraft that would fold up and stow away. If it had not been for the unfortunate accident that befell her, she surely would have contributed more.

When the French submarine *Surcouf* was apparently lost in an accidental collision off Panama, the allied fighting powers lost a remarkable boat. At 2,880 tons, she was a giant by the standards of the day and would have posed a serious threat to enemy shipping during the Second World War.

The Italians, Russians and Poles all carried out feasibility studies on using aircraft with submarines, but none ever carried out experiments combining the two. We come finally to the American contribution, from their reasonably successful MS-1 Martin aircraft in the early 1930s to the Regulus missiles that were first launched in the 1950s. The Americans carried the experiments further than anyone else and, as recent as 1965, the Rand Corporation carried out a feasibility study on a design for an aircraft that could travel both under the water and above.

With the arrival of the British Aerospace Harrier, or the McDonnell Douglas AV8B as it came to be known in the USA, I think the spark may have been rekindled and there are now greater possibilities of using submarines as underwater aircraft carriers. It is hoped that this book will keep alive some of the ideas and dreams of some of the world's great aircraft designers.

Terry C. Treadwell

Regulus missile being launched from the fantail of the submarine USS *Helena* (CA-73). (USN)

The French submarine *Surcouf* leaving harbour.

Acknowledgements

When I first contemplated writing, then re-writing this book, I did not realise the daunting task that lay ahead, but encouraged by my wife Wendy and friends Captain Richard C. Knott, USN (ret.), Captain Ted Wilbur, USN (ret.), and Ed Heinemann (now sadly deceased) who was kind enough to write the foreword, I finally crossed the last 't' and dotted the last 'i'.

I would like to thank the following:

Roy Grossnik, Head of the USN History Office, who unhesitatingly offered me all the facilities of his department; Dr. Dean Allard of the USN History Office who dug deep into the archives to find some of the superb photographs in the book; R.D. Layman who allowed me to use some of his own archive material; 'Schone' Schonenburg and Lois Lovisolo, formerley of the Grumman History Office (now defunct), for supplying me with photographs and additional information on the Loening XSL-1 and Captain Richard C. Knott, USN, former Editor of Naval Aviation News, who was a constant source of encouragement. Also Margaret Bidmead and the staff of the Submarine Museum at Gosport. Their archives hold some of the most fascinating material on submarines to be found anywhere in the world. And last but not least; Alan Wood, John Batchelor, Bruce Robertson and any others I might have forgotten to mention.

Terry C. Treadwell

Introduction

This book is about the use of aircraft on submarines and the disasters that dogged their development.

The initial idea was born during the First World War, when the German Imperial Navy placed a Friedrichshafen FF29 across the bows of the U-2 submarine and headed for the coast of England. The attempt was a partial success, but like all progressive ideas there are those regressives who think they are a waste of time. The Imperial German Naval hierarchy was no exception and ordered that the trials cease. The British Admiralty also attempted to use the submarine as an aircraft carrier, by placing two Sopwith Schneider seaplanes across the stern of the E-22 submarine. Like the other attempts, they too were only partially successful and it was considered not to have any real merit so the idea was dropped.

In the 1920s, Britain again took the idea on board and converted the M-2 submarine by removing the eight inch gun housed in front of the conning tower, and replacing it with a watertight hangar that housed a specially designed aircraft, the Parnall Peto. Trials went well, but then came a tragic accident that resulted in the loss of the submarine and her entire crew.

The Americans too investigated the idea, but with limited success. They tried a variety of aircraft and although they never had any serious accidents, the idea was dropped when news came of the British disaster.

The idea was to lie dormant for a number of years, but then came the Second World War. 'Necessity,' they say, 'is the mother of invention', and the Second World War nurtured this in no uncertain way. One of the ways, was that the idea of carrying aircraft on submarines was again considered a distinct possibility. The Japanese created a number of different types of submarines that were capable of carrying aircraft, from the I-15 that carried just one aircraft to the I-400 class that could carry four fighter-bombers.

The French too had developed a giant submarine, the *Surcouf*, which through a number of disasters, none of which was connected to the design of the submarine or the aircraft it carried, was lost under mysterious circumstances off the Caribbean. The Germans made their contribution in the meantime, by developing a small rotorcopter that was used as an observation aircraft towed behind a U-boat.

In Poland, they were carrying out experiments with an aircraft that could be carried aboard a submarine, but like so many others it drifted into obscurity. The Italians went as far as even producing the aircraft that would eventually be carried aboard one of their large ocean-going submarines, but the demise of the submarine itself put an end to that idea.

The only real success of the submarine borne aircraft was when a Sieran fighter bomber from the Japanese submarine the I-15 successfully bombed the forests of Oregon in the United States – twice. In the latter stages of the war, Japanese aircraft-carrying submarines massed near Panama with the intention of attacking the Gatun Locks there. They were discovered and attacked by carrier aircraft before they could carry out the attack and the war ended before another attempt could be made.

The Americans never lost sight of the idea and developed it by putting missiles like the Regulus I and II in hangars aboard submarines and launching them. We all know the result that that development produced, and today we have submarines that are bigger than most warships, carrying up to thirty missiles that have more destructive power than the combined forces of the Second World War ever had or envisaged. The submarine-borne aircraft of the First World War and Second World War were not the success their innovators would have hoped, but they set the stage for the modern missile carrying submarines of today.

1　The Early Years

A little over eighty years ago, a handful of officers in the Imperial German Navy began to look into the possibilities of operating aircraft from submarines, although at that time there was no operational requirement to do so. Rather, it was a case of personal initiative, circumstance and the availability of a Friedrichshafen FF 29 twin-float, single-engined seaplane.

During the early stages of the First World War the German Army quickly overran Belgium. As a result the port of Zeebrugge was soon in German hands, becoming a base well suited to operations by U-boats. The base commander, and U-boat captain, Oberleutnant zur See Friedrich von Arnauld de la Periere, who also and unusually, happened to be an aviator, together with Oberleutnant zur See Walter Forstman, commander of the U-12 (both later to become 'Ace' U-boat commanders), were seized with the offensive spirit. Determined to find out whether the radius of action of a seaplane could be usefully extended by using the submarine as a seaplane transporter, they set about finding out. The nearest point on the enemy coast, North Foreland in Kent, lay some seventy-three miles away.

Despite it being midwinter, on 6 January 1915, the seaplane, with its 57ft wingspan, was lashed down athwartships to the foredeck of the U-12 and the unlikely pair sailed out into the harbour to carry out trials. The bows were trimmed down and the aircraft was subsequently floated off and taxied away – all within the protection afforded by the long breakwater of the Zeebrugge Mole. It was decided to continue with the trials immediately. The strange and vulnerable combination, with the aircraft lashed athwartships and the U-12's two heavy Korting oil engines leaving a tell-tale plume of smoke, headed for the open sea. Despite a heavy swell, the situation was about manageable.

Some thirty miles offshore, the U-boat's commander flooded the forward tanks and released the aircraft which was able to take off successfully. With von Arnauld de la Periere and his observer Herman Mall aboard, they flew along the coast of Kent undetected before returning to Zeebrugge direct, rather than making the agreed rendezvous with the U-12 in weather which had deteriorated further. At the debrief, Forstman and von Arnauld considered the whole exercise a complete success but agreed that after the difficulties in getting the aircraft launched, the seas needed to be calmer and the aircraft more secure on the deck to prevent serious damage or loss of life.

This remarkable trial conducted in wartime, virtually in the enemy's backyard, was designed to establish a strike capability with small bombs, if not at the

Friedrichshafen FF 29 No.201 aboard a German U-Boat. To launch the aircraft, the bow section of the submarine was submerged and the aircraft floated off.

Friedrichshafen FF 33H aircraft carrying out tender trials.

heartland then at least the coastal towns of the enemy. Soon the Friedrichshafen FF 29 had been adapted to carry 12kg bombs, and during the year, twenty-six raids were flown against British and French targets. On Christmas Day 1915, a Friedrichshafen FF 29 flew along the River Thames to Erith on the outskirts of London and dropped two bombs. It was fortunate that they fell without causing injury and damage. Three British aircraft chased the FF 29 without success and it returned safely. The German airmen or 'Zeebrugge Flers' as they were called, had more problems from their aircraft than they did from the British. On many occasions their seaplanes were forced to land with fouled ignitions or fuel-line stoppages and because of the limited range of their aircraft. As a result, many of the more important targets were beyond reach. Understandably, the frustrations of the aircraft crews created morale problems. These problems were recognized by the U-boat officers because they also shared the dangers of operating relatively new and untried weapons. Because of this a bond sprang up between them.

Combined trials of aircraft and submarine had continued sporadically, but high level support was not forthcoming. No doubt this was a correct decision given the vulnerability of the combination and the unreliability endemic in these early aeroplanes. A report to the German High Command on the future of submarine-launched aircraft was thoroughly investigated and the decision was made that the project be dropped. Von Arnauld was told,

> 'U-boats operate in the sea, aircraft in the air – there is no connection between the two'.

On the other side of the English Channel the British were experiencing serious problems with their air defences against the German Zeppelin airships which could outclimb any of the aeroplanes of the period. Further, the air defences were in no way integrated. The army's Royal Flying Corps and the navy's Royal Naval Air Service each seeking its own solutions to the German menace. The navy believed that the role of an aircraft-transporting submarine should be for use in surprise interception when an enemy airship was making its run toward the coast, low down. In fact, the British carried out a raid on Christmas Day 1915 on the German Zeppelin sheds. Seven aircraft were launched from three separate surface ships. Although their mission only met with partial success, it was in fact the world's first 'carrier' attack. It was this partial success that prompted the Admiralty to consider other methods of launching aircraft.

It had been noted by ships in the English Channel that the Zeppelins flew very low until they approached the English coast where they climbed sharply and headed inland. The idea of using a vessel to transport a number of seaplanes out into the Channel was that they could surprise the Zeppelins before they had time to climb to their bombing height. With this in mind, the 660-ton submarine E-22 was dry-docked and two parallel ramps fitted. These extended from just behind the conning tower to the end of the upper deck casing. On 24 April 1916 the

E-22 submarine having launching rails fitted to her stern.

submarine was taken to NAS (Naval Air Station) Felixstowe and two Sopwith Schneider twin-float, fighter seaplanes, borrowed from NAS Felixstowe, were hauled aboard by means of trimming the stern and floating the aircraft on. The E-22 carried out two practice runs in the North Sea near the Heligoland Bight. This was the area in which the Britain-bound Zeppelins were most likely to be encountered.

The first attempts to launch the aircraft were disastrous. After the E-22 had trimmed down at the stern and the two aircraft floated off, the notoriously weak floats of the Sopwith Schneiders broke up in rough water just before take-off. After a few more attempts and a number of temporary repairs, both aircraft were able to take-off and returned to Felixstowe. The diminutive Schneider was unsuited to rough water operations and although the aircraft were launched on a couple of occasions, as far as can be ascertained, no interception of a Zeppelin by a Schneider was ever made. The idea was good but impractical and the loss of the E-22 and her log, which would have given more information on the trials, put paid to any more thoughts of combining aircraft and submarine.

The E.22 was on patrol in the English Channel on the 25 April 1916, when at 11.50 a.m. she was struck by a torpedo from the German submarine U-18. There were four survivors but only two lived, Engine Room Artificer F.S. Buckingham and Signalman Harrod. Both managed to stay afloat on pieces of wood from the deck platform that was fixed aft. This platform supported the two Sopwith

Schneider seaplanes that were normally carried, but they had been taken off that morning. After the survivors had struggled in the water for about one hour and a quarter, the German submarine U-18 surfaced and picked them up. They were interned in Holland for the duration of the war.

The point of these events lies not in the detail, but in the realisation that in two years of war, naval officers of the two major naval powers engaged in the conflict had explored the potential of a crude combination of submarine and aircraft both for offensive strike and for defensive interception. Perhaps at first the most obvious role, reconnaissance, appeared to have been neglected. This in fact was not the case; for a submarine to have its own built-in airborne reconnaissance capability would require greater sophistication by many orders of magnitude.

Following the end of the First World War, more than twenty years of experimentation were to be needed before one nation, Japan, solved the problem to the point where over-ocean reconnaissance missions could be flown as routine, to yield useful results in war. Experiments and development trials are one thing; but operational use with its basic requirements for repeatability is quite another.

One German who had continued to consider the problem was Dr Ernst Heinkel who, in 1917, produced the first tiny aeroplane designed for dismantling and stowing aboard a new class of ocean-going submarine then undergoing construction. The first prototype aircraft, the Brandenburg W20 flying boat (navy number SN-1551) first flew in 1917. The Brandenburg Company had a contract

The Hansa-Brandenburg W20/2 on its beaching trolley.

to deliver three experimental aircraft, of which the first had cantilever wings. The lower wing, which was only 20ft long, was mounted on top of the fuselage, while the upper wing was supported by two pairs of struts that ran from the fuselage sides to a point about mid-span on the underside of the top wing. The wing design was not structurally strong enough and the aircraft crashed into the River Havel on its initial flight.

The second of the aircraft was redesigned with a new strut arrangement and a new wing design which was much stronger. This time it completed all of its flight tests successfully and set the standard for the third and last of the W-20's. Although the W-20 could be assembled in less than three minutes and disassembled in about the same time, its actual flying performance left a lot to be desired. Powered by a seven-cylinder Oberursel Rotary engine of 80hp, it took over fifteen minutes to climb to 3,000ft. Considering it only carried enough fuel for a seventy-five minute flight, this really was not very impressive. The aircraft could be stowed in a pressure-resistant container measuring 20ft by 6ft. As it turned out the Brandenburg W-20 never completed the full trials, as no U-boats could be spared.

In 1916, as part of the British Emergency War Programme, four K Class steam powered submarines K-18, K-19, K-20 and K-21 were being built, when it was decided by the Submarine Development Committee to cancel the building of these K Class boats and build Monitor Class submarines. As only the keels had

British K boats tied up at Portsmouth

been laid, it was decided to use all the materials planned for the K boats in the construction of M boats. It is not true that K boats were converted into M boats, because the hull form of the M Class was completely different to that of the K's. The M Class submarines were big boats for their type.

Towards the end of 1918, trials were carried out by the British Admiralty with the steam turbine submarine HMS K-5. It was fitted experimentally to tow an SS-Zero type blimp that carried an observer, enabling the blimp to extend its cruising radius for the protection of the convoys against German U-boats. The experiment was extended later that year to 'C' class submarines, which were used for towing kite balloons with an observer aboard, in an effort to spot U-boats beneath the surface. It was never a success.

The same year, a German company, the Luft Fahrzeug Gesselschaft or Air Travel Company, put forward a design for a single-seat scout plane. The LFG V19, or Putbus, as it was called, was a long wing monoplane built of aluminium and powered by a 110hp Oberursel rotary engine. The V19 was a very simply designed aircraft, of which the fuselage was just a tube of flat wrapped duraluminium. The wings held all the fuel and had automatic shut-off valves that enabled the wings to be removed without first draining the tanks.

Weighing 1,056lb empty and with a wingspan of 31ft, the Putbus could reach a speed of 112mph. Although initially the V19 Putbus appeared to be better than the W-20, this was proved not to be so. The main problem was that it took ten times longer to assemble and disassemble, and required five waterproof containers to house it. The German Navy's submarine arm was told that it was ready for trials, but then shortly afterwards came defeat for Germany and all such trials and experiments were shelved.

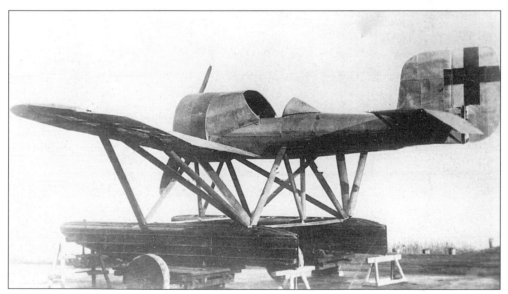

The LFG Roland V19 'Putbus' on its launching trolley.

Friedrichshafen FF29 taking off after being launched from the U-12 .

Sablatnig SF.3 being lifted aboard the submarine U-12 during trials.

Kapitänleutnant Walther Forstmann of the U-12.

Korvettenkapitan von Arnauld de la Periére (second on left,) commander of the U-12 submarine, with members of his crew.

The Hansa-Brandenburg W20 in water.

Head-on view of the Hansa-Brandenburg W20/1.

Close-up of a Sopwith Baby floatplane having just been floated off the stern of the E-22.

E-22 with two Sopwith Schneider floatplanes on her deck.

E-22 submarine with one Sopwith Schneider on stern, the other having been floated off just rear of the stern. (J.M.Bruce)

The stern of the E-22 submarine being submerged to enable the remaining Sopwith Schneider to be floated off. (J.M.Bruce)

The two Sopwith Schneider aircraft, having been launched from the E-22 submarine, taxi away to start their trials. (J.M.Bruce)

2   The Interwar Years

As war reparations, German submarines became available to Japan for evaluation. While there is no evidence of any German trial evaluations of aircraft aboard submarines in the closing stages of the war, with either the Heinkel design or the slightly later L.F.G. Straslund V19, Dr Ernst Heinkel continued to work in secret on his intended submarine-based design. There was a need for secrecy because the Allied Air Control Commission forbade Germany to construct any military aircraft after the First World War.

Dr Heinkel designed and developed an all-plywood biplane called the Heinkel-Caspar U-1, which could be dismantled and stowed away in a small 24ft by 6ft cylinder. When being dismantled the fuselage was supported by a small crane mounted on the deck of the submarine. By opening a small door under the tail section, a lever was pushed forward causing the wings to unlock. The wings were then placed on a dolly along with the fuselage and floats, which had been removed when the aircraft's fuselage had been supported by the crane. The whole thing was then wheeled into the cylinder ready to be removed and reassembled when required.

After long and exhaustive tests, the U-1 was manufactured at a works owned by a former German naval pilot, Carl Caspar, at Travemunde on the Baltic (delivery being completed by 1923). The United States Navy and the Japanese Imperial Navy, who incidentally were allies at this time, were so impressed with the little Heinkel-Caspar U-1 that they ordered two each. It would be interesting to know how the aircraft were described to the Allied Air Control Commission when they were sold, considering Germany was forbidden to build any military aircraft. Possibly, they were sold as simple reconnaissance aircraft, but even they have a military connotation. In any event the orders were completed in 1923.

The details of the many dismountable trials aircraft produced between the wars, with a few exceptions, do not form part of this book. Most suffered from a combination of a lack of robustness for repeated operation and poor performance not least due to their small size. Others had varying degrees of unsuitability because of the time taken to assemble them or take them apart again for stowage in a watertight compartment on the deck of the parent submarine.

Under the constraints of peacetime budgets, aircraft development went ahead slowly. The US Navy, however, persisted. From 1919 to 1933 it tested designs bought from Grover Loening, Heinkel Caspar, Glenn Martin, Cox Klemin and the Martin Company – not to be confused with Glenn Martin.

In 1919 the US Navy purchased three small monoplane seaplanes from

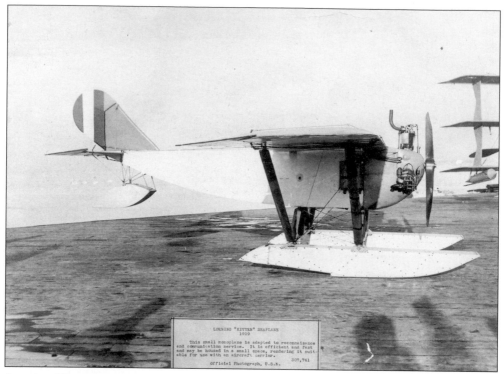

Loening 'Kitten' experimental seaplane. Side view. (USN)

the Loening Aeronautical Company. They were called M-2 Kittens and were given the US Navy designations S/N A442 to A444. The aircraft were designed for quick assembly and disassembly, and for storage aboard a submarine. At a time when nearly all American aircraft were biplanes, the Loening Kitten was revolutionary. It was a high-wing monoplane, whose wings were supported by aerodynamically shaped struts. Weighing less than 300lbs it was the smallest aircraft ever built for the US Navy. The engine for the first test was an all-British Corporation 30hp air-cooled, two-cylinder Lawrence but, although designed and built specifically for the Loening Kitten, it was replaced by the Americans without reason. The trials of all three aircraft were not very successful, but they gave sufficient information for the US Navy to enable them to insist on certain specifications when ordering three more experimental aircraft from the Martin Company.

The three aircraft ordered were in fact a development of an even smaller aircraft design that had been built as experimental lightweight fighters for the US Army Air Service. They were given the naval designations of S/N A5840 to 5842 KF-1. It is interesting to note, that J.V. Martin, although accepting the contracts, did not have a factory of his own but sub-contracted the project out to a company called Gaullaudet. The US Navy liked the aircraft, but decided against the whole project and cancelled the order. They stated that while the parent craft remained

The J.V.Martin KF-1 taxiing in after flight trials.

comparatively small, submarine-based aircraft were likely to prove little more than toys. Should, for other purposes, requirements exist for submarines of large displacements, then aircraft for operation from them could be designed to more sensible parameters. Until requirements existed for large submarines in quantity, even successful trials made with one-off trials submarines could at best only be a precursor.

The Japanese were starting to show an interest in the idea when, in 1919, they purchased seven war-prize U-boats from the German Imperial Navy, with the intention of adopting the best features into the designs of their own submarines. Two years later they purchased two Heinkel-Caspar U-1 aircraft, but it was in 1927 before trials had been completed. By this time the Japanese had developed their own aircraft, the Yokosho 1-go, based on the U-1 but with one or two modifications and a more powerful rotary engine. This aircraft was operated from their submarine the I-5 for eighteen months, but was too slow and was transferred to the I-51 Class submarines in 1930. A number of new innovations were made during the initial period, with the result that the I-51 had a compressed-air catapult fitted to her afterdeck, together with a hangar capable of taking two aircraft. The aircraft chosen was the Yokosho E6Y1 Type 91 Reconnaissance seaplane, which was almost identical to the British Parnall Peto, powered by the 130hp Armstrong Siddeley Mongoose engine. The Peto had been successfully tested aboard the ill-fated M-2 submarine. The first successful testing of the Yokosho E6Y1 (J-52) was in the May 1928, from the submarine I-51. Subsequent tests in 1930 and

Yokosuka Type 1, a Japanese copy of the German U-1. (USN)

Japanese submarine I-51 is seen here as submarine No.44 before her conversion.

Yokosuka E6Y1 converted for use aboard submarines. (Bob Mikesh)

1931 were successful and the the aircraft was officially adopted as a reconnaissance seaplane for the submarine fleet.

The US Navy revitalised their interest in the concept in 1922, when they too ordered the purchase of two twin-seat, twin-float, all-wood folding Heinkel-Caspar U-1's from Germany. The two aircraft, designated A 6434 and A 6435, were received at NAS Anacostia at the end of 1922 after previously being inspected by a Lieutenant Commander Zachary Lansdowne, USN. Lansdowne was to lose his life three years later, when the airship he was commanding the, USS *Shenandoah*, came apart in the air during a cyclonic storm.

The Heinkel-Caspar was an incredible little aircraft, in as much as no tools were required to assemble or disassemble her. One of the most unusual features, was that the engine could be crank-started from inside the cockpit. This was a great deal safer than having a man straddled across the floats swinging the propeller. Unfortunately before they could be used, one was lost during an exhibition flight and what was left was used as spares for the remaining one. By the beginning of 1923, all the flight tests had been completed, but the Navy decided to use the information gained to build their own design.

They put out two contracts with strict specifications, one to the Cox-Klemin Aircraft Corporation and the other to the Glenn-Martin Corporation. Twelve aircraft were ordered, with six coming from each company. The Cox-Klemin aircraft were made of wood and the Glenn-Martin aircraft made of aluminium. This allowed the Navy to compare the use of different materials.

The tests were carried out at Hampton Roads, Virginia, during October and November 1923 using the submarine USS S-1. The submarine had a complement of aircraft specialists from the USS *Langley* aboard under the command of Lt Cmdr V.C. Griffiths. Their job was to assemble and disassemble the Glenn-Martin MS-1 and the Cox-Klemin XS-1 as they were known, then stow them away in a pressure-resistant tank aft of the conning tower. Unfortunately it took nearly four hours to assemble and disassemble the aircraft. This was obviously unacceptable and so both aircraft were sent to the Naval Air Factory in Philadelphia for modifications to be carried out. The aircraft were delivered to the factory in late December 1923 but it was to take nearly two years before the modifications were completed.

The first flight of the XS-2, as it was known after modification, took place on 28 July 1926 and was flown by Lt Dolph C. Allen. The flight was uneventful and the aircraft landed alongside the S-1 submarine and taxied upon the partially submerged, slanting, aft portion of the deck. After trials lasting four months, the deck crews could assemble the XS-2 in twelve minutes and disassemble her in only thirteen minutes. Despite the success of these trials, the project was shelved. The

Loening 'Kitten' experimental seaplane. Front view. (USN)

Pilot climbing into the cockpit of the Loening Kitten.

The Caspar U-1 being tested at the Naval Air Station Anacostia, Washington. The capitol building can be seen faintly in the background.

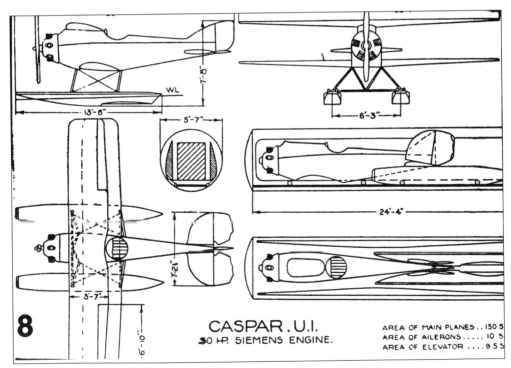

Plan drawing of the Caspar U-1 powered by a 30hp Siemens engine.

The Martin MS-1 submarine-launched seaplane. This tiny seaplane was stowed inside a hangar built into the conning tower and allowed the captain of the submarine to send out a spotter aircraft in search of potential targets.

Cox Klemin XS-1. This aircraft had a wooden frame and floats and was started by means of a handcrank in the cockpit.

Aircraft XS-2 being readied for launch aboard the USS S-1. (USN)

Close-up of the hangar aboard the USS S-1. (USN)
Following pages: Martin MS-1 aboard the submarine USS S-1 (USN)

Close-up of the MS-1 aircraft aboard the USS S-1.

The Martin MS-1 flying over the USS S-1 after successfully being launched. (USN)
Opposite: The hangar door is lowered to reveal the MS-1 aircraft inside. The bottom
picture shows the little aircraft partially assembled. (USN)

The Martin MS-1 being recovered by the USS S-1, after a successful launch. Note how the stern of the submarine is partially submerged so that the seaplane can float on. (USN)

The USS S-1 surfacing in the New Thames Estuary to launch the Martin MS-1.
Previous pages: The MS-1 being assembled aboard the submarine USS S.1.

main factor behind the decision was the length of time the submarine had to stay on the surface during the launch and recovery procedures.

While the USA were experimenting, by the late 1920s, Britain, France and Italy were at last at the first stage of having one big submarine each, either in commission or projected.

In Britain's case the submarine HMS M-2 was an M Class submarine of 1,600 tons surface displacement, and had been designed to be fitted with a 12-inch gun. Although the keel was laid in 1916, the M-2 was not completed until 1920. The construction of the M Class submarines – or 'Mutton-boats' as they were sometimes called – had come about after four K Class submarines, that had been ordered as part of the Emergency War Programme in 1916, had been cancelled. As only the keels had been laid, it was decided to use all the materials planned for the K boats, for the construction of the M boats. The M class submarines were big boats for their type being 305ft long, 24ft 6in deep and 15ft 9in wide. Surface displacement was about 1,600 tons and underwater displacement approximately 1,950 tons. They were powered by two sets of twelve cylinder diesel engines, giving a combined total of 2,400hp and electric motors that gave 1,500hp. The maximum surface speed was 15.5 knots and 9.5 knots was the submerged speed.

The main feature of the M class submarine was the 12-inch gun that was mounted forward of the conning tower. The gun was one that had been previously intended for the pre-Dreadnought battleships of the King Edward VII class. The shell fired by the gun weighed 520lb, which corresponded roughly to the 550lb bomb used by the RAF. The procedure for firing the gun was carried out by means of a manoeuvre called a 'Dipchick'. It was fired from the control

Side view of the M-2 submarine before it was converted to carry an aircraft.

room after the submarine had been brought up to periscope depth and the muzzle of the gun was just above the surface. The muzzle had an electrically-operated watertight muzzle cap that was opened just prior to firing. The submarine then surfaced, fired its gun and submerged again, the total time taken to carry out this procedure being just forty seconds. The only problem was that the submarine had to surface again to re-load. Although the gun was unable to traverse, it was able to elevate to thirty degrees. It was said that the accuracy of the big gun was extremely good, but it was never fired in anger. In fact there is no record of it having ever been fired.

The subsequent Washington Naval Treaty forbade guns of a calibre greater than 8in on board submarines, whereupon the M-2 had its 12in gun removed and was converted to carry an aircraft – the work being completed by the Spring of 1928. An extract from a report to the Lords of the Admiralty in 1930 read:

> The function of the aircraft is to increase the range of vision of the submarine and so remove the very considerable handicap under which submarines normally labour in this respect; to act in fact as an additional and very powerful periscope.

The role of the M-2 submarine was seen by the navy as an unseen scout for the fleet. It would cruise a considerable distance ahead of the fleet, then surface to launch her scout plane. The aircraft would then fly even further ahead, searching for enemy battleships and radio back any scouting information. Using the submarine as a submersible aircraft-carrier, it reduced the chance of being discovered, therefore giving the fleet the edge in a possible confrontation. A mission such as this required a submarine aircraft-carrier to have a high speed and a long range – the M-2 had all these requirements.

Parnall Aircraft had secured the contract for the aircraft, to be named the Peto after one of the former captains of the M-2, a Lieutenant Commander Peto, who it is said co-opted Parnall into the design. The first Parnall Peto was displayed at the Seventh International Aero Exhibition at Olympia, London, in 1929. The fuselage was constructed of spruce wood and steel tubing and covered with a mixture of fabric and aluminium panels. The wings were made entirely of spruce and covered with fabric, while the fin and rudder frames were made of stainless steel and covered in fabric. With a wingspan of 28ft 5in that folded to only 8ft it was a most compact aircraft. Powered initially by a 135hp Bristol Lucifer IV engine, this was soon replaced with an Armstrong-Siddeley 'Mongoose' engine of the same horsepower. When fully loaded the aircraft weighed 1,950lb, had a maximum speed of 113mph and an endurance of about two hours.

The aircraft trials, initially flown by Lieutenant C.W. Bias and Lieutenant C. Keighley-Peach, proceeded in peacetime at a pace which may appear leisurely to outsiders. But to those engaged on them, and who are accustomed to proceeding smoothly from one crisis, major or minor, to the next, time

Parnall Peto taxiing alongside the M-2 after launch trials.

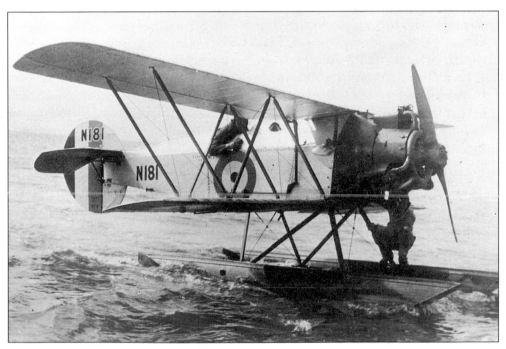

The Parnall Peto about to start taxiing trials.

passes all too quickly. The launch sequence of the aircraft would start while the submarine was still submerged. There was a crew of five who manned the hangar, including two from the Royal Air Force. They would enter the watertight hangar through a hatch that was connected to the conning tower. One inside the hangar space was at a premium, therefore each member of the crew had his own station. The electric heaters in the aircraft would be turned on to pre-heat the oil in the engine and crankcase, enabling the engine to be started the moment the aircraft was clear of the hangar. As the submarine surfaced, the hangar door would be lowered to form part of the launching platform. The Parnall Peto would then be pushed out on its launching trolley and connected to the steam catapult, which launched the aircraft at a pressure of 825psi. The pilot and observer would then climb aboard while the wings were being unfolded and locked into position. With the engine started and taken up to full power, the captain of the submarine would head the boat into wind and increase speed. When the pilot was ready, he gave a wave of his hand and the catapult officer would release the aircraft – subjecting the crew to a 2.7g launch. The aircraft would be at flying speed in less than 40ft, the whole operation taking less than five minutes (the fastest time was four minutes) from the time the submarine surfaced. The two pilots assigned to the M-2 for the initial seaborne trials, were Lts Villiers and Keighley-Peach. Both were in the unique and enviable position of receiving both flying and submarine pay.

Recovering the aircraft, except for the catapult sequence, was virtually a reversal of the launch. After flying trials had been completed, the Parnall Peto would land on the water and taxi alongside the submarine. The crane mounted on top of the hangar would then be swung out and the hook lowered onto a ring mounted on the upper wing. The aircraft was then raised out of the water, swung inboard and lowered back onto its launching trolley. The pilot and the observer would than exit and the wings would be folded back allowing the aircraft to be pushed back inside the hangar.

During one of the flying trials, the Peto buzzed the coast in Stokes Bay near Lee-on-Solent, Hampshire, and was involved in a rather unusual accident. It appears that the aircraft unaccountably lost height as it was flying low over the beach – some say because of an eighteen stone, overweight observer by the name of Lieutenant Couper. After narrowly missing a row of beach huts, the tip of one of the aircraft's floats caught the last one causing the aircraft to crash. Not only did the collision cause extensive damage to the aircraft, but it totally destroyed the beach hut, leaving a prominent local citizen, a Dr Lampblough, standing amidst a pile of rubble in a state of total nudity. The good Doctor then proceeded to verbally abuse the pilot and his observer, who although unhurt, were trapped beneath the wreckage of the aircraft. They in turn asked him to stop swearing and assist in their release. It was only when a crowd started to gather that the man realised that he was still naked. Suffice to say, he was not amused and contacted the Rear-Admiral (Submarines) at Portsmouth almost immediately. There were rumblings through the corridors

. . . Sorry old chap; Not enough lift in the air!

A cartoon of the incident in 1926 when the M-2's Parnall Peto crashed into a beach hut, somewhat annoying its occupant.

of the Admiralty very soon afterwards. It is said the only person to receive any sort of punishment for the incident, was the commanding officer of the M-2 submarine who was not only replaced, but lost a well-earned promotion. His replacement, Lieutenant Commander John Duncan de Mussenden Leathes, was to enjoy his new command for only a short time. Both the pilot and observer were also replaced, by Lieutenants H.C. Topping (pilot) and C.R. Townsend (observer).

A number of the early trials of launching and recovering of the aircraft were carried out in the Mediterranean during the summer months of 1931. This was done because of the calm seas that usually were inherent in the area during this period. The submarine operated out of Gibraltar and carried out a number of successful dives.

Just after 0900 hours on the morning of 26 January 1932, M-2 left Portland to link up with other submarines from the 6th Flotilla off Portland Bill on routine exercise. The M-2 radioed the depot ship HMS *Titania* routinely at 1011 hours that she was about to dive in West Bay, off Portland, Dorset, at around 1030 hours. This was the last communication that anyone ever had with submarine

M-2. By lunchtime the radio operators aboard HMS *Titania*, reported that radio contact had been lost with M-2, but it was considered that there was no real cause for anxiety as it was probably due to a communications problem and would rectify itself in due course. But by 1616 hours, when the M-2 should have reported back to Portland, the mood had changed. Search vessels were immediately sent out to comb the area in the hope of locating the submarine. Later in the day, during one of the search sweeps, the Admiralty received word from a Captain A.E. Howard of the Newcastle coaster *Tynesider*, that he had seen a large submarine diving stern first, which as most people know is not a recognised diving manoeuvre carried out by submarines. This was the last time that the M-2 was seen on the surface. It appears that Captain Howard was outward bound from Charlestown to Graveline, France, with a cargo of china clay aboard, when at 1115-1120 hours as he approached Portland, he saw a large submarine with the letter 'M' on its conning tower no more than 800 yards from his ship. After watching her for about ten minutes, the submarine suddenly started to submerge stern first, the fore feet and the bow being the last parts to disappear. Captain Howard stated that he did not see anyone on the bridge or on the deck while it was on the surface, nor did he see anyone in the water after the M-2 submerged.

Later that evening as the *Tynesider* left Portland after bunkering with coal, Captain Howard saw a submarine approaching and it was this vessel that he had thought he had seen earlier. Much later that evening he heard on the ship's radio that the submarine M-2 was missing, it was then that he contacted the Admiralty. A submarine officer was immediately sent to interview Captain Howard, taking with him photographs of the M-2 submarine. The submarine was identified immediately as being the missing M-2. The Admiralty announced that evening:

> News has been received this evening that submarine *M-2* dived at about 1030 this morning off Portland, and since then no further communication has been received from her. Destroyers and submarines from Portland are searching the area in which she was last known to be, and every endeavour is being made to establish communication with her.

But Captain Howard was not the only person to see something that day. Captain Hunt, master of the vessel *Crown of Denmark*, was approximately half a mile from where Captain Howard had seen the M-2 dive, when at around 1840 hours, he saw a bright flash of light on the port beam. Ten minutes later he heard two loud explosions, he investigated but saw and found nothing on the surface.

Four other people also saw something in the bay that day. A party of three ladies and a gentleman were motoring on the top of Portland Bill, which overlooks West Bay, at 1400 on 26 January and said they saw a submarine cruising in the bay. When interviewed at a later date by a submarine officer and shown photographs of the M-2, they immediately identified it as the one they saw in West Bay. As the M-2 was the only submarine carrying out trials in West Bay that day, there can be no mistake about which one it was. The only other explanation, is that another submarine coming in from the English Channel on its way to Portland came across West Bay. If so, this could possibly be the one that the captain of the *Tynesider* said he saw when he was leaving Portland after bunkering with coal. It is the discrepancy in the times that gives rise to concern. The captain of the *Tynesider* says that he saw the submarine M-2 submerge stern first at 1130 hours, while the party of men and women on Portland Bill, saw the submarine at 1400 hours on the surface. There is obviously some mistake in the times as there has never been any suggestion of a cover-up, nor is one suggested.

In the early hours of the following morning the Admiralty announced that:

> An object presumed to be the M-2 has been located three miles off Portland in seventeen fathoms (102ft) and on a sandy bottom. Salvage craft and divers have been sent from Portsmouth to this position with the utmost dispatch.

The salvage craft was HMS *Sabre*, a destroyer that carried divers who had been specially trained for deep-sea work. She was later joined by two other salvage ships. These ships, and others sent from Portland, patrolled the West Bay with their echo-sounding gear, in the hope of detecting any tapping sounds that might be coming from the trapped crew. A number of sounds were said to have been heard, but none were confirmed.

The object that had been located, turned out to be an old wreck. The problems facing the searchers, was that a large number of wrecks littered the sea bed in the West Bay area, which was known locally as the 'Bay of a Thousand Wrecks'. Every time the sweep wire snagged on something, there was no way of telling what it was until divers had gone down to investigate. The search became long and painful and all the time the chances of finding somebody alive diminished by the hour. Time was now of the essence and the sweep continued day and night, the divers working by the light of underwater lamps. By now the divers were becoming exhausted and they realised that the chances of finding the crew alive was more and more remote, but still the operation continued.

Then, on 2 February, a fisherman reported that he had caught the body of a man dressed in dark trousers and white sweater (this was the standard dress for submariners) in his nets, but was unable to pull the body aboard and consequently lost it. The search ships continued to sweep the sea bed with cables, then suddenly a cap and collar was brought to the surface which was identified as belonging to the coxswain of the M-2. The search crews knew that they were getting close. The next day, the destroyer HMS *Torrid* located what they thought was the M-2 and shortly afterwards two mine-sweepers, HMS *Pangbourne* and HMS *Dunoon*

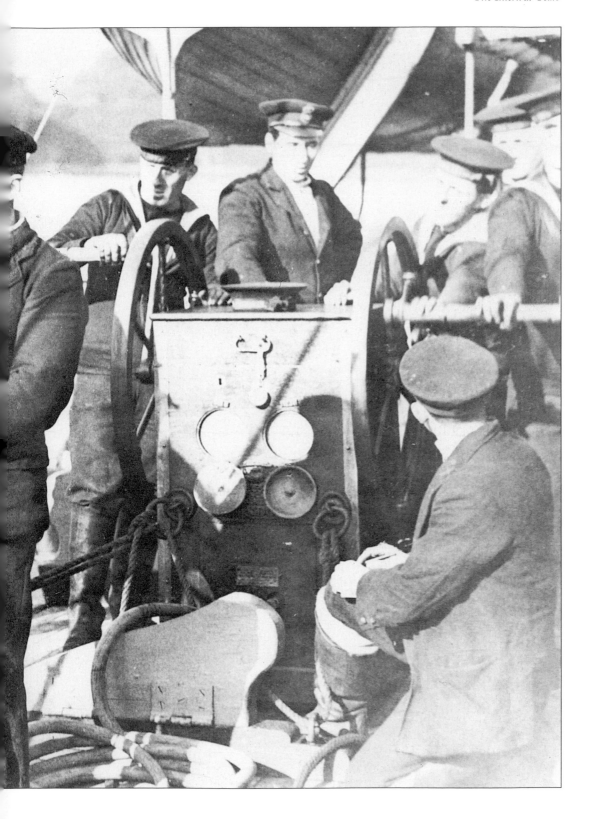

The crew of the M-2 submarine. The two RAF members of the crew are standing at either end of the back row.
Previous pages: A salvage diver about to descend on the M-2 after it had sunk off Portland.

arrived and sent down divers. It was only when one of the divers saw the letter and number 'M-2' on the side of the conning tower that they were able to confirm that it definitely was the submarine. The Admiralty immediately issued a communique:

> The Rear Admiral Submarines has reported that the M-2 submarine has been located 50 deg.31.2 min N., 5.8 miles from Portland Bill.

The official description on how the wreck was found, was attributed to the Asdic listening equipment aboard the destroyer HMS *Torrid* and confirmed by divers. It was an extremely difficult task for the divers because of the limited visibility and the very strong tides and undertow in the West Bay area. The M-2 submarine was in 106ft of water, listing about 150 degrees to starboard, with her stern embedded in the sandy bottom, but with her bows well clear. So clear in fact, that the divers were able to walk beneath the bows. They also noted a large groove in the sea bed directly under the rudder, which extended aft for a short distance. The Admiralty announced later:

> Diving operations on the M-2 up to date, have revealed that the hangar door and upper conning tower hatch are open and that

the forward hatch and engine room hatch are closed. It has not yet been ascertained whether the lower conning tower hatch, the hatch inside the hangar giving access to the interior of the submarine are closed or open. It has been decided that the salvage of the M-2 is to continue, weather permitting.

It was also noted later that the access hatch from the hangar into the submarine was wide open; the portable launching rails were not in position; the bridge telegraphs to the engine room were both at stop and the fore and aft hatches could be raised by divers, meaning that they were unlatched on the inside. All voicepipes from the control room to the bridge were shut off, but the voicepipe from the hangar into the submarine was open.

By now though it was realised that it was too late to save any of the crew and the only thing that remained, was the possible salvage of the submarine. The Admiralty accepted the services of Ernest Cox, a civilian salvage expert who had purchased the scuttled German Fleet at Scapa Flow in 1924 and had raised a number of the ships, including the 28,000 ton battle-cruiser *Hindenburg*. He planned to clamp patches over all the apertures on the M-2, then pump it full of compressed air and blow her to the surface. Divers continued to dive on the M-2 and discovered that besides the hangar door being wide open, the hatch between the hangar and the hull of the submarine was also open as was the conning tower hatch, but the forward and aft deck hatches were closed.

Five weeks later it was discovered that while the salvage crew were preparing to raise the submarine by blowing the air out of her, it was found that the main ballast-tanks were interconnected, so that it would be impossible to blow out one tank at a time. This meant that the tank-side blow-valves inside the submarine were open, which in turn meant that the M-2 was in fact blowing her tanks while in the process of surfacing, but had not reached full buoyancy when the incident had occurred.

This new information gave more weight to the theory that the submarine was in the process of carrying out a rapid surfacing exercise so that the aircraft could be launched quickly. Submarine officers who knew the commanding officer, Lieutenant-Commander J.D. de M. Leathes, stated categorically that he was not the type of officer who took needless risks and would not have lowered the hangar door until the submarine was settled on the surface. The fact that the conning tower hatch was open, they said, was proof that either he or someone else was on the bridge watching the launching operation.

Because the M-2 submarine was a heavy boat and that it took over a quarter of an hour to blow all her main ballast-tanks to give her maximum buoyancy, it was never laid down that launching procedures for the aircraft should be delayed until the ballast-tanks were completely empty. The agreed method was to hold the submarine on the surface by means of the hydroplanes, while the tanks were being blown then carry out the aircraft launch procedure.

There are three possible theories as to what happened to the M-2 and theories are all they can be, because no one will ever no for sure what happened on that fateful day when the entire ship's company of sixty officers and men, including two Royal Air Force mechanics, were lost.

The theories are as follows:

1. In an attempt to carry out a rapid launch sequence of the scout aircraft, the submarine would be driven upwards and forwards on her propellers with her hydroplanes set to rise while her ballast tanks were still being blown. The intention would be to get the hangar door clear of the surface and lowered while the hydroplanes held the submarine on the surface. If there had been a hydroplane failure while the aft ballast tanks still contained water, then the submarine would have settled back rapidly beneath the surface. Any hatches open, such as the conning tower hatch, would rapidly cause water to cascade into the boat, making it virtually impossible to close any hatches.

2. If the vent valves to the aft ballast tanks had inadvertently been left open, then they would start refilling the moment the M-2 surfaced. At the moment of surface, the captain would have climbed onto the bridge and upon realising what was happening, would have ordered the vents to be shut. By this time the stern would have sunk well below the surface and the hangar door, which would probably have been open, would have started shipping water and caused the submarine to rapidly sink – stern first.

3. The third, and most likely, possible cause was that the accident occurred during a practice launch, when the hangar door was opened too soon. If this had happened and the access hatch between the hangar and the pressure hull were open, water would have rushed into the hangar and into the submarine forcing her down.

If the hydroplanes had failed to hold the M-2 on the surface while the hangar door was open and the water had started to come into the hangar, the position of the hatch between the hangar and the submarines hull might hold the key to the accident. The hatch was of a projecting tube construction 2ft 6in above the deck positioned in a narrow passageway that ran down the starboard side inside the hangar and tucked in the corner over a pump. Under normal conditions it was an extremely awkward position to get to and, under adverse condition such as a large rush of water coming into the hangar, almost impossible. With the hatch open and a large rush of water coming in, the water would have flooded down into the control-room and onto the main electrical switchboard and fuses, immediately rendering all electrical equipment inoperative.

Why there were no survivors was another question that was asked a number of times, especially considering that the submarine carried the Davis escape apparatus. In all probability it was a combination of circumstances. With the water pouring in from the hangar and from the conning tower, the crew would

Parnall Peto being hauled up the slipway after being recovered from the wreck of the M-2.

have had very little time – if any at all – to don their 'lungs'. The extremely cold water (after all, it was the middle of January) would have had the effect of slowing the men down, and had any escaped to the surface, there was no ship up there to rescue them as no one knew they were missing.

Three months later, on 18 March, divers recovered the body of Leading Seaman Albert Jacobs from the cockpit of the Parnall Peto in the M-2's hangar and brought it to the surface. Jacobs had been a member of the aircraft launching party. The aircraft was recovered by divers by fitting steel hawsers to her and pulling her out of the hangar and to the surface. She was badly damaged in the process and her remains were put onto a lighter and taken back to Portland.

Then, on 1 July, a second body, that of Leading Aircraftsman Leslie Gregory, RAF, dressed in a flying suit, was recovered from the seabed lying fifteen feet away from the submarine near the port-side rudder. The recovery of these two bodies and the circumstances in which they were found supported the theory that a launch was in progress. There followed nearly a year of extremely hazardous salvage operations, including at one point raising the submarine to within eighteen feet of the surface, but the M-2 was lost when a gale sprang up and a hawser snapped. The submarine slid back down on to the seabed and was then left as a grave, a tribute to the brave officers and men who gave their lives in the formative years of the submarine service. Ten months after the M-2 had

The Parnall Peto after being recovered from the M-2.

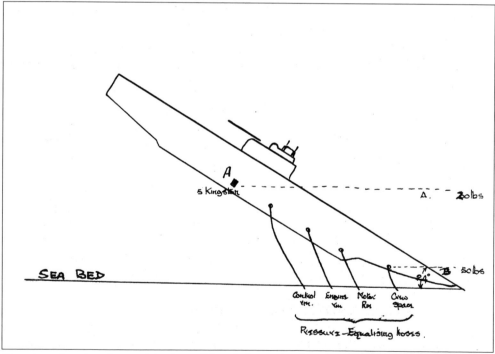

Drawing showing the positioning of the air hoses in the attempt to raise the M-2 during abortive salvage attempts.

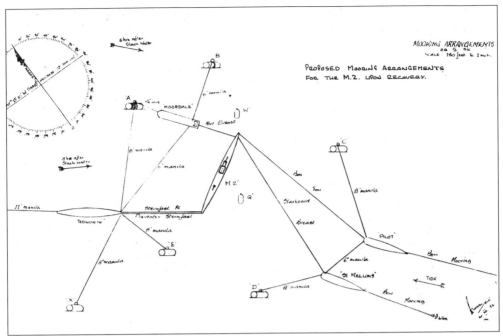

Drawing showing the complex mooring arrangements planned for the M-2 after salvage.

left Portland on that fateful day, the Admiralty announced: 'It has been decided finally to finish salvage on the M-2.'

The loss of the M-2 resulted in the Admiralty ending all trials between aircraft and submarines. This took the form of a message sent to the Rear Admiral (Submarines) commanding Gosport:

M.02285/32 21st October

Rear Admiral (S)
HMS Dolphin
Gosport

With reference to your letter No.613/S.97/B.1 of the 3rd September 1932, I am to inform you that their Lordships concur in the proposal that trials of aircraft working with submarines should now be abandoned. The Air Ministry will be so informed.

BY COMMAND OF THEIR LORDSHIPS.

The last remaining Parnall Peto was sold to the Japanese Imperial Navy. This purchase was to prove fruitful for them in future years.

The Parnall Peto was not the first British aircraft destined for use on a submarine.

The Bristol Burney X3 on sea trials.

In 1916, two Sopwith Schneider seaplanes were carried aboard the E-22 submarine, lashed down on the deck. Even earlier, well before 1914, an aircraft called the Bristol-Burney X3 was built. The Burney had been the brainchild of Lieutenant C.D. Burney, RN, who had been impressed with the work the Italians had been carrying out with hydrofoils. The intention was to employ hydrofoils and water propellers on the lower end of the legs, which, when powered together with the aeroplane's 200hp Canton-Unné engine, would propel the airplane through the water at a speed that would enable it to alight from the water more easily than one with floats. The X3 had a wingspan of 57ft 10in, was 36ft 8in in length, had a wing area of 500 sq.ft and carried two people. It was designed to collapse and pack away on both surface vessels and submarines. While the X-3 enjoyed some success, like its predecessors, the X1 and X2, it too was wrecked and destroyed during launching trials.

A further design was put forward in 1939 using the Type X-1 submarine, but it got no further than the drawing board. Although based loosely on the M-2, the hangar was situated vertically in the deck, as can be seen in the drawings opposite.

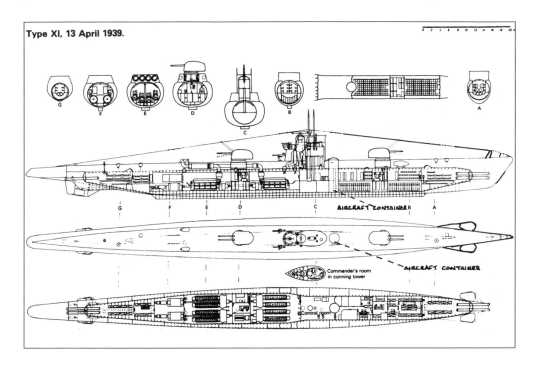

Type XI, 13 April 1939.

Above and below: Diagrams showing the layout of the aircraft storage aboard the Type X-1 submarine.

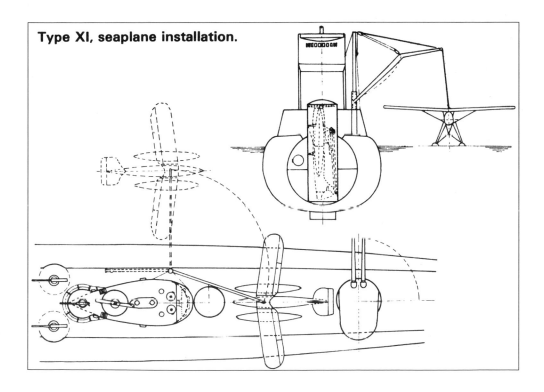

Type XI, seaplane installation.

A Fairey III aircraft taxiing towards the L-8 submarine on tender trials.

The M-1 submarine painted in dazzle camouflage, seen here during high speed trials.

The X-1 submarine, the forerunner of the M-2.

The X-1 submarine.

The M-2 submarine after having its 12in gun removed during its conversion.

The M-2 being launched after its conversion to an aircraft-carrying submarine.

The M-2 submarine on trials after its conversion.
Opposite: Close-up of the aircraft catapult equipment on the M-2.

The Parnall Peto on the slipway. This became the standard aircraft for use with the M-2.

The M-2 about to carry out diving trials after conversion.

The Parnall Peto in the hangar on the deck of the M-2.

Overhead shot of the Parnall Peto out of the hangar with one wing extended.

Close-up of the Parnall Peto outside the hangar of the M-2 with one wing extended.

Above: The Parnall Peto being prepared for launching. The wings are being secured into position by RAF and RN crew members.

Excellent bow shot of the M-2 with its Parnall Peto on the catapult.

A shot taken from inside the
hangar on the M-2 as its Parnall
Peto aircraft is launched.

Below: M-2 submarine
launching its Parnall Peto
float-plane.

Parnall Peto taxiing to the M-2 after its launch trials.

Starboard view of the M-2 recovering the Parnall Peto after trials.
Opposite: A head-on view of the Parnall Peto being hoisted aboard the M-2.
Previous pages: Port-side view of the M-2 recovering the Peto after trials.

Above: The M-2's Parnall Peto on its beaching trolley.

A poor quality shot of the pilot of the Parnall Peto getting into the cockpit. This view was taken from inside the hangar of the M-2.

M-2 lowering the Parnall Peto into the water while in Gibraltar harbour.

Parnall Peto aircraft taxiing away from the M-2 submarine after being lowered into the water. The submarine is berthed alongside the quay in Gibraltar.

The M-2 submarine alongside the quay at Portland. The propeller of the Parnall Peto seaplane can just be seen inside the hangar.

Below: The Peto is hoisted after salvage from the wrecked M-2.

Above: Stripped remains of the Parnall Peto aircraft after it had been removed from the sunken submarine M-2.

The two RAF crew members of the M-2 On the left is Leading Aircraftsman Leslie Gregory while on the right is Leading Aircraftsman Harman.

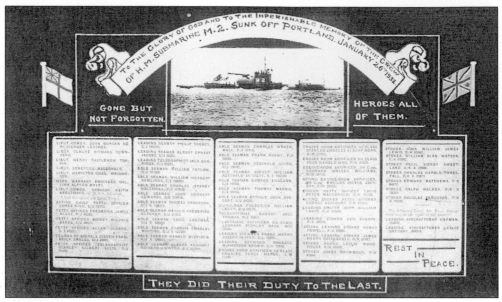

In memory of the gallant crew of the M-2.

M.02285/32.   21st October   2

Rear Admiral (S),
    H.M.S. DOLPHIN,
        Gosport.

                    With reference to your letter
No.613/S.97/B.1 of the 3rd September, 1932, I am to
inform you that Their Lordships concur in the
proposal that trials of aircraft working with
submarines should now be abandoned.   The Air
Ministry will be so informed.

                        BY COMMAND OF THEIR LORDSHIPS,

The Admiralty telegram that confirmed the end of British submarine aviation trials.

3   The War Clouds Gather

The end of the First World War had left the warring nations economically exhausted. To bolster their already depleted fleet, the French decided it would be cheaper to build submarines than conventional warships. Contrary to the Washington Naval Treaty of 1921, the French embarked on the construction of a number of 1,500 ton submarines with a range of 10,000 miles and capable of a surface speed of seventeen knots.

Meanwhile, in 1922 the French Admiral Drujon, drew up plans for a fleet of giant commerce-raiding submarines and submitted them to a naval commission for consideration. After a number of setbacks and a variety of alterations to the original plans an order was placed for the first of these giant boats to be built at Cherbourg. She was to be named the *Surcouf* after Robert Surcouf, a French pirate who became the scourge of the Indian Ocean and the British Navy in the 1800s.

In November 1929, France launched *Surcouf*, commissioning her in 1933. *Surcouf* was a giant for her day, 330ft long (compared with the M-2's 296ft) and 28ft in the beam. She had two 203mm guns mounted in a water-tight, power-operated turret, two 37mm cannons, two Hotchkiss machine guns and ten torpedo tubes, four of which were mounted internally, the remaing six on a platform mounted on the stern. She also had a reconnaissance aircraft in a hangar on the deck. The aircraft, a Besson MB-411 AFN floatplane, was small, simple and of modest performance, as was the M-2's Parnall Peto. What could be done with slightly later technology aboard a parent craft of a similar order of size will be revealed later.

Attached to the 5th Submarine Flotilla, *Surcouf* carried out a series of sea trials, each one becoming longer in duration. The longest trial being across the Atlantic to the Caribbean, returning via North Africa, a distance of some 16,000 miles, nearly all of it on the surface. There were problems almost from day one. The most serious was that it took about $2\frac{1}{2}$ to 3 minutes to submerge the boat to a depth of 40ft, whereas the conventional submarines of the time could reach this depth in twenty-seven seconds. She also became very hard to control while underwater and with over twenty buoyancy vents to adjust, trim was very hard to set. As a result, on a number of occasions this caused serious problems to the safety of the boat and its crew.

Despite these problems, the *Surcouf* was at the time the world's largest, most powerful and best-armed submarine. She continued her peacetime career by, among other things, trialling her first aircraft, the Besson MB-35 Passe-Partout (named after the Jules Verne character from *Around the World in Eighty Days*). The aircraft had been introduced to the French Navy in 1926 for use aboard cruisers, but had been discarded for an improved and more powerful version, the MB-410. The construction of the MB-35 was ideal for storage in small places and seemed to be what was required for the submarine. It was a long-wing monoplane with a tail that extended beneath the fuselage rather than above it. Both the fabric-covered wings and tail folded flat against the side of the fuselage, also covered in fabric, and could be assembled and disassembled in a matter of minutes. It was powered by an uncowled 120hp Salmson radial engine. Trials were carried out with the MB-35, which was launched and recovered by crane, only to be replaced after crashing by a second improved version called the MB-411 in 1935. This too crashed during the trials. A second prototype was ordered, but the Marcel-Besson Company had gone bankrupt and the contract to provide the aircraft was given to ANF Les Mureaux.

The new aircraft was fitted with a more powerful engine, the 175hp Salmson 9AD radial. Although similar in construction to the original prototype, it had a cowled engine, a large centreline float and two small wing floats. Initially built as a single-seat aircraft, after acceptance trials on *Surcouf*, it was converted to a twin-seat. The aircraft had a wing span of 39ft 4in and a length of 27ft. The maximum speed was 115mph while its normal cruising speed was 81mph. Normal range was 215 miles, but if flown as a single-seater and with an auxiliary fuel tank fitted in the observer's seat, it had a range of over 400 miles. It remained in service and was on board *Surcouf* when, after the fall of France in 1940, the submarine went to Plymouth to join the Free French Forces of General de Gaulle.

The Italians had also been carrying out trials with the submarine the *Ettore Fieramosca*, which had been designed by Bernardis of the Regina Marina built in

A model of the *Surcouf*.

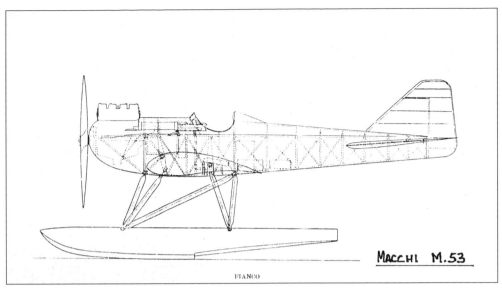

FIANCO

MACCHI M.53

Side-view plan drawing of the Macchi M.53.

1926 by the Cantiere Navale Franco Tosi, in Tarranto. A competition was held in 1927-1928 to select an aircraft that could be carried on the Fieramosca and two were submitted – the Macchi M.53 and the Piaggio P.8, both powered by the ADC Cirrus II engine. A single aircraft of each type was built, serialled respectively MM.94 and MM.95, at a cost of 215,000 lire each. Although ostensibly ordered by the Regina Marina, the aircraft were to be operated and flown by the Regina Aeronautica (Royal Air Force). The aircraft trials were successful and came up to all expectations, but they were never trialled aboard a submarine.

The submarine *Ettore Fieramosca* on the other hand was not a great success. It was classed as an ocean-going boat and entered service with the Regina Marina in 1930. During the Second World War it served with the 11th Squadron of the 1st Submarine Group and was based at La Spezia. It only carried out three complete cruises with a total of thirteen days at sea. The second of her missions while in Southern French waters, was marred by an explosion in her batteries which required extensive repairs. The repairs caused the submarine to be re-assigned to training duties as she was considered not fit for active duty and was eventually struck from the list on 10 April 1941.

Also in Europe in 1929, Jerzy Nikol, a graduate from Warsaw Technical University, was working on the design of a two-seat light amphibian flying boat. It was a labour of love rather than one of commission, and was carried out slowly in his spare time. It came to the attention of the Polish Navy and in 1934 when a new warship, the ORP (Okret Rzeczypospolitej Polskiej or 'Ship of the Polish Republic') *Gryf* was being built a proposal was put forward to fit a catapult on the ship and use the Nikol A-2, as it was now called, as a reconnaissance aircraft. Jerzy Nikol submitted his proposals for the project, but after lengthy discussions

Polish submarine *Orzel* - front starboard three-quarter view. (USN)

it was decided not to fit the catapult. However, the navy still retained interest in the aircraft.

After extensive tests, including the making of a scale model of the aircraft for wind tunnel tests at the Warsaw Aerodynamic Institute, and the submitting of detailed designs and calculations for approval by the IBTL, construction of the A-2 prototype began at the Morski Dyon Lotniczy's workshops at Puck, Poland, in 1936. The thinking behind the navy's interest at this time, was to consider using the little flying boat on a submarine. Many tests with aircraft on submarines had been carried out in a number of countries with some degree of success, so it was decided to carry out an in-depth survey into the possibilities of marrying up the little aircraft with the submarine *Orzel*, one of the large ocean-going submarines of the Polish Navy.

The A-2 was a two-seat, cantilever wing, monoplane, light amphibian flying boat made entirely of wood. The wing was constructed of a number of watertight compartments which enabled the aircraft to stay afloat, even if there was considerable hull damage, and was attached to the hull by four bolts. The wing-tip floats were of wooden construction attached to the wings by means of steel tube struts. The cockpit area was situated in front of the wing and consisted of two side-by-side seats with dual controls. The adjustable in-flight tailplane, with twin rudders, was mounted on a pylon over the rear end of the plywood-covered fuselage. All the fixed surfaces were covered in plywood and the movable surfaces in fabric. The partially retractable landing gear was fitted with brake-equipped wheels. Only the upper ends of the compression legs were retractable and they raised the wheels above the water. Powered by a 130hp de Havilland Gipsy Major four-cylinder, inverted inline, air-cooled engine, which drove a three-bladed, wooden, pusher airscrew, the Nikol A-2 made a large number of test flights. The results from these tests showed that the aircraft had excellent handling qualities both in the air and in the water. Unfortunately there was only one A-2 and at the outbreak of the Second World War it was destroyed in a bombing raid.

Although the use of aircraft on submarines had been temporarily shelved in the United States, interest still remained. In 1929, fresh life was breathed into the project, when Dr Grover C. Loening started fresh talks with the US Navy Bureau of Aeronautics with the idea of producing a fold-away aircraft. How he managed to persuade the board to accept his idea after they had turned others down, no

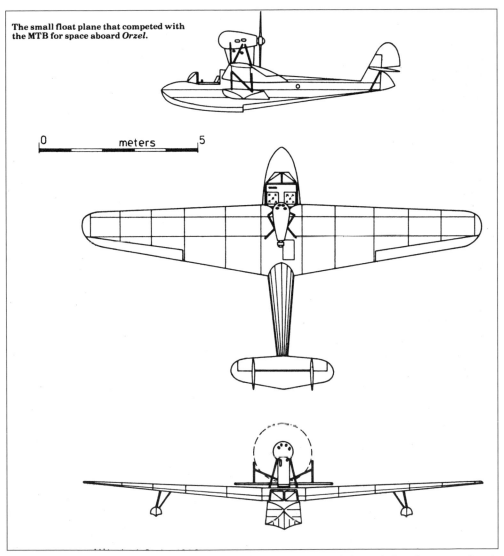

The small float plane that competed with the MTB for space aboard *Orzel*.

0   meters   5

Plan drawing of the Nikol A-2, designed to be carried aboard the Polish submarine *Orzel*. (USN)

one will ever know, but it was accepted and a contract was negotiated. Using his knowledge of previous attempts at building such an aircraft, Dr Loening decided that it would have to be a seaplane and not a floatplane. It had to be capable of being assembled and disassembled by the minimum amount of men – four was the ideal number because of the narrow deck of the submarine – in less than five minutes. Because of the short time required to assemble the aircraft, it would have to be of the simplest of designs and have very few parts. The aircraft met all the requirements, but it carried only enough fuel for one hour of flying time. It also carried a small, specially constructed, lightweight radio transmitter and receiver, and a Very-light pistol. It wasn't a very fast aircraft but it did have a good rate of climb.

The US Navy ordered the XSL-1 (XSL stood for Experimental Scout plane manufactured by Loening), which after purchase was given the designation of S/N A8696. The navy were impressed by the way the Loening XSL-1 folded up for stowage with the minimum of loose parts. First the stabilisers and elevators folded downwards together, then the entire tail assembly folded forward on hinges that were fixed to the top longeron onto the aft hull deck. All the wing brace struts were connected to thirteen structural members by a single five-eighth-of-an-inch bolt. When the bolt was removed, it allowed the wings to be unhooked from the hull. The wing brace struts then folded onto the upper surfaces of the wings leaving the

The American Loening XSL-1 experimental aircraft in the Wind Tunnel Test Facility at Langley Field.

entire power-plant nacelle to fold down onto the aft hull deck. All that was left to do, was to hook the wings onto brackets on the hull and push the aircraft into its hangar.

Flight tests were carried out by a Mr Allison Gillies at North Beach Airport (now La Guardia) and on completion of the Navy's inspection and acceptance trials, it was decided to fly the aircraft to the Anacostia Naval Air Station, Philadelphia. On the day before delivery, the Delaware River froze and it was decided that the aircraft would have to be transported by road to Washington. The first journey to Washington was very nearly its last. The aircraft was dismantled and packed into a large removal van and, at midnight the same day, the unlikely cargo left North Beach, New York. James C. Reddig, who was the Deputy Chief Engineer of Loenings at the time, takes up the story:

> The van's route was through Queensborough Plaza at the eastern end of the Queensborough Bridge to Manhattan. This particular area, was a focus of transportation and had been under construction for a number of years. It was a maze of supports for elevated subway lines and barricades for roadway rebuilding and surface car tracks. A pattern that changed daily in a confusion of red warning lights.
>
> The driver of the big van failed to make a sharp enough turn and had to back up for a second try. In doing so, he backed through a barricade. The rear end of the vehicle dropped into an excavation, open all the way down to the underground subway beneath and coming to rest at about a twenty degree angle. The van's contents were not adequately braced for this type of manoeuvre and slid backwards against the rear doors. They were held from bursting open only by a light slack chain that was looped through the door handles. Loose items and tools escaped through the partially open doors and fell onto the subway tracks below. More important was an exhausted and rudely awakened mechanic by the name of John Sullivan who, wrapped in a mover's blanket, had elected to travel with the aircraft. Pinned in amongst the jumble, Sullivan had the presence of mind to remain still in the darkness when he heard the shouting of rescuers. The power was shut off, leaving trains and travellers trapped for about an hour. All sorts of emergency vehicles and personnel arrived and block and tackle was swiftly rigged from the elevated train structure overhead to hold the van and prevent it falling further. With the help of cranes and trucks, they managed to extricate the van from its precarious position.

In the meantime, an access panel had been hammered open at the forward end of the van and a light and rope lowered to lift a bewildered and somewhat frightened John Sullivan from his unhappy predicament. The van was returned to North

Beach, where inspection showed the aircraft to have suffered some minor damage from its rough treatment. The navy granted Loening a three week extension of delivery date for repairs.

The necessary repairs having been made, the XSL-1 carried out flight tests on the Anacoastia River, but as Dr. Loening had calculated, the bulky wing brace struts created airflow interference when the aircraft was near the stall. The XSL-1 was then flown to Langley Field by Lt. Perry, USN, for tests in the new NACA (National Advisory Committee for Aeronautics) full-scale wind tunnel. This was the first time an aeroplane had been tested there using smoke for flow studies. While at Langley the XSL-1 was flight tested by Melvin N. Gough the NACA test pilot. His report is as follows:

NATIONAL ADVISORY COMMITTEE
FOR AERONAUTICS
LANGLEY MEMORIAL AERONAUTICAL LABORATORY
LANGLEY FIELD, HAMPTON, Va.
October 5, 1931.

MEMORANDUM for Engineer-in-Charge
Subject: Report on XSL-1

In regard to the flight characteristics of this airplane, the following were noted:

1. The stabiliser was to the end of its full up range at its leading edge. The elevators, and particularly the ailerons, have large frictional forces which do not permit a good test of stability.

2. The take-off was reasonably quick, requiring approximately eight to ten seconds. (The water was but very slightly rippled).

3. On the climb the airplane was tail heavy to such a degree that release of forward-stick pressure allowed the nose to rise so rapidly as to give the impression of longitudinal instability; and the higher the nose got, the less effective were the elevators, and the large forward-stick movements were necessary to cause slow nosing over.

4. The rate of climb was estimated at around 600 to 700 feet per minute and the high speed close to 100 miles per hour.

5. The change in balance due to power change was never noticed. Sudden reduction of power, even when expected, caused such a nosing up that correction for it could not be effected without a bump in the flight path.

6. Longitudinal stability was the next studied, but the airplane could not be flown level or in a power-off glide at any speed hands off; the tail heaviness started the upward oscillation which rapidly rotated the airplane to a high angle and caused a rapid reduction in air speed and nosing-over control effectiveness. This would be quite dangerous in the event of power-plant failure near the water, particularly on take-off.

7. The lateral stability was not investigated because of the control friction.

8. Directional stability was not investigated because there may be wing heaviness and aileron deflection with resultant yawing moments.

9. Turns are quite difficult to execute properly with the airplane in its present condition, since 'tightening up' is more difficult to determine than rising of the nose on the horizon.

10. The glide is quite steep with a high rate of descent and much like that of the McDonnell. Levelling off and landing consisted of decreasing the forward-stick force to level off and then constant forward movement to check the rotation and to keep the position above the water as speed is lost and the angle of attack is increased until the airplane finally settles on the water.

11. With the pilot in the cockpit the airplane was balanced on the handling gear and the C.G. located at approximately 40 to 50 per cent of the chord from the L.E.

12. Before the balance is changed but after the control friction is decreased I would like another flight to determine:

(a) Wing Heaviness
(b) Directional, lateral and spiral stability.
(c) Possibly to allow the airplane to come up to the complete stall if permission is granted,
to   chance the possibilities of airplane spinning. This condition is known from
other reports   to be had, and the impression gained by the pilot is that since the rate of
increasing angle   and decreasing of checking control are so fast, if the stall was reached the
controls would   e very slow in effecting recovery if at all useful.
(d) Evidence of buffeting.

13. If the balance is corrected, another flight would definitely fix the longitudinal stability.

> *Melvin C. Gough*
> *Associate Test Pilot.*

After all tests had been completed, the XSL-1 was accepted by the Navy, subject to certain redesign features being carried. There were a number of changes made, among them was the recently made-available Menasco 145hp 'Buccaneer' inverted, six-cylinder, air-cooled engine that was used to replace the fold-down Warner engine. The advantage was that the Buccaneer engine could be left in situ and only the propeller needed to be removed. As the whole essence of the submarine-aircraft relied on speed of assembly and disassembly, it was necessary to have a speedy means of removing the

Loening XSL-1 experimental seaplane. Side view. (USN)

propeller. It was decided to use a powerful differential screw nut instead of the hub nut already on the Hamilton Standard propeller. The engine starting handle was adapted as a spanner and used for undoing the nut quickly. Once removed, the propeller was stowed in a well set in the hull beneath the engine. The redesigning completed, the aircraft was designated the XSL-2. In Washington, the office-bound pilots used the XSL-2 to get in their flight pay requirements. It soon became a firm favourite with them because of its delightful handling qualities.

Authorization was then given to design a watertight hangar for the XSL-2 and this was probably under construction when the tragic news of the British submarine, the M-2, reached America. Because no satisfactory explanation was given about the accident at the time, and because of the adverse publicity given to the accident by the press, the US Navy decided it would 'cool' its interest in the project.

Up to now all the demonstrations of the XSL-2's stowage capabilities had been carried out in a hangar on an outlined deck space. The four-man team, through continuous practice, were able to fold the aircraft in fifty-six seconds and unfold it with the engine ready to start in fifty-nine seconds. One wonders how they would have fared on the deck of a submarine in a heavy swell. No doubt the time would have been considerably longer. It was the easy folding and unfolding, that was to spell disaster for the XSL-2. In the spring of 1933, the Anacostia River rose to an unusually high level and flooded the airfield and the hangars.

The XSL-2 was normally parked in a hangar on its beaching trolley in a folded configuration. The other aircraft in the hangar were landplanes and as such, just sat in the muddy waters, easily cleaned up after the floods had receded. But the XSL-2's hull was boat shaped, consequently the aircraft floated up with the engine weight topside, the result being that the XSL-2 turned over and sank. The damage was extensive and the Navy, after looking at the estimates, decided that the cost of repairing the spot-welded, stainless-steel structure and generally overhauling the experimental aircraft, could not be justified. It was therefore decided that the whole project would be quietly abandoned.

There is one point worth mentioning however. Many aviation historians believe that the XSL-1 was in fact a rebuilt version of the 1930 Loening 'Duckling', an experimental, commercial flying boat. To help put the record straight, the misunderstanding arises from the fact that both hulls were built on the same jig, making the external boat-lines identical. The difference was that the 'Duckling's' hull had been partially covered with thin Westinghouse 'Micarta' cotton-filled phenolic sheets, whereas the hull of the XSL-1 was all aluminium built to the specifications of the US Navy.

Loening XSL-2 experimental aircraft in a folded configuration.

During the 1930s Japan was the only major power to make significant progress with submarine-aviation, following the purchase of the British Parnall Peto and the acquisition of German war-prize submarines and two Heinkel-Caspar U-1 miniature seaplanes. However, in Russia, Igor Chetverikov, a designer for the state-owned TsKB (Tsentral'noe Konstruktorskoe Byuro – Central Design Bureau), was beginning the preliminary designs of a small submarine-borne, reconnaissance flying boat. The Soviet navy started to express an interest in the project, but by this time Igor Chetverikov had been transferred to the NII GVF (Nauchno-Issledovatel'skii Institut Grazhdanskii Vozdushnii Flot) facility where he went to work for the OSGA (Experimental Aircraft Manufacture for Civil Aviation). It was to them that an order was made for a prototype of the aircraft that Igor Chetverikov had been earlier concerned with. Designated the OSGA-101, the aircraft was primarily to be used as a flight-test vehicle. It was a three-seat wooden monoplane, with tubular steel booms extending from behind the cockpit area, upon which twin tail surfaces were fitted. The engine, an M-11 of 100hp, was mounted on a pylon just behind the cockpit, while the undercarriage was manually retractable. The first test flights took place in the spring of 1934 and the results were both encouraging and useful.

It was then decided to produce a second model, designated the SPL, which was designed specifically to operate from a submarine. Although only marginally smaller than the OSGA-101, the SPL could be folded to fit inside a cylinder (hangar) 24ft 5in in length and 8ft 2in in diameter. It was of a very simple design, constructed for ease of assemble and disassembly. The wings swivelled and folded

Chetverikov SPL in assembled configuration – side view.

Chetverikov SPL in folded
configuration – head-on view.

aft against the fuselage, while the pylon-mounted engine folded down atop the
fuselage. The whole procedure took only four to five minutes to assemble the
aircraft and three to four minutes to disassemble and stow it away. The flight
tests were better that expected. but the hydrodynamic qualities left a great deal to
be desired. Consequently the Soviet navy lost interest and the aircraft was given
to the Osoaviakhim, who re-designated it the GIDRO-1. It was later exhibited at
the Milan Air Show of 1936.

The Japanese continued to make progress and based the design of their largest
submarines on the German U-142, a 2,160 ton UA cruiser that had been built
in November 1918. Two of these were built, each with hangars for two aircraft,
a compressed-air catapult and a crane for aircraft retrieval. It may be said that in
1935 the first aircraft produced in any quantity intended for operation on board
submarines was born. It went into production the following year.

The Watanabe E9W1 Type 96 Model 11 was a small two-seat reconnaissance
floatplane like its slightly earlier Western contemporaries, but its Hitachi
GK2 Tamput engine gave 340hp, almost twice that of the Salmson in the
French MB-411 for example. A significant step-up in performance was under
way. Four prototypes of the E9W1 were produced followed by thirty-two
production aircraft. These, aboard their parent submarines, were used to seek
out Chinese ships attempting to run the blockade during the Sino-Japanese
conflict of the late 1930s. By December 1941, when Japan made her surprise

attack on the US bases in Hawaii, the Japanese Imperial Navy had eleven submarines in service capable of carrying aircraft. By the end of the Second World War she would have twenty-seven.

It was in 1941 that the large cruiser submarines of the I-9 to I-12 Class came into service. They carried the Watanabe E9W1 and had a long range (16,000 miles at 16 knots). The I-11 was fitted out as the squadron flagship and carried extra communications facilities. In 1942, changes were made in the I-11's engines that reduced her power from 12,400hp to 4,700hp, with a loss of speed from 24 knots to 17 knots. However, as the new engines were smaller and weighed less, fuel capacity was increased by 37 tons and the cruising range became 22,000 miles at 16 knots. Also in 1941, the first monoplane to be carried aboard a submarine made its appearance. It was the E14Y1 or as it became known to the Allies, the *Glen*. Manufactured by the Kyushu Aircraft Company (formerly the Watanabe Aircraft Company), 126 of these aircraft were made within the next two years. Unfortunately not one has survived.

The Glen differed to all the other submarine-aircraft built up to that time. She was a low wing, two-seat monoplane, powered by a 340hp Hitachi radial engine. Manufactured of a combination of metal and wood, she had her wings and fuselage covered by fabric and metal panels. Wooden wing ribs with metal spars were used to strengthen the detachable wings and the cockpit had a sliding canopy for both pilot and observer. It was this aircraft that carried out the reconnaissance over Pearl Harbor before and after the infamous attack in December 1941. This aircraft type was to become the eyes of the Japanese submarine fleet.

There were very serious problems at first in preparing the aircraft for launch and recovery. It took nearly an hour languishing on the surface to launch or recover these reconnaissance aircraft and, on a number of occasions, the aircraft had to be abandoned when the submarine crash-dived after being threatened by either approaching aircraft or surface vessels.

The *Surcouf* during sea trials. A good shot of the twin 8in guns. (USN)

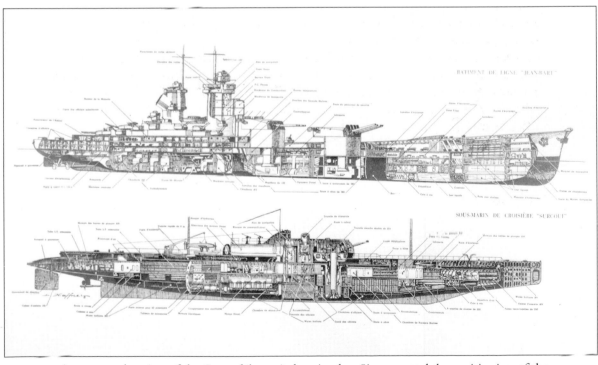

A cutaway drawing of the *Surcouf* (lower) showing her 8in guns and the positioning of the aircraft storage.

A close-up of the model showing the Besson aircraft aboard the *Surcouf*.

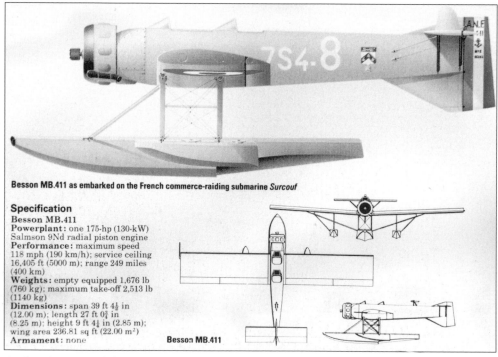

Besson MB.411 as embarked on the French commerce-raiding submarine *Surcouf*

Specification
Besson MB.411
Powerplant: one 175-hp (130-kW)
Salmson 9Nd radial piston engine
Performance: maximum speed
118 mph (190 km/h); service ceiling
16,405 ft (5000 m); range 249 miles
(400 km)
Weights: empty equipped 1,676 lb
(760 kg); maximum take-off 2,513 lb
(1140 kg)
Dimensions: span 39 ft 4½ in
(12.00 m); length 27 ft 0¾ in
(8.25 m); height 9 ft 4¼ in (2.85 m);
wing area 236.81 sq ft (22.00 m²)
Armament: none

Besson MB.411

A plan drawing of the Besson MB.411.

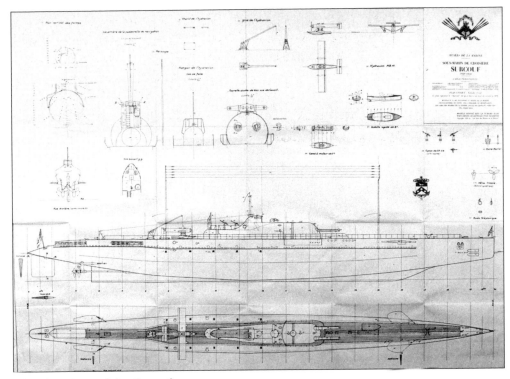

Plan drawings of the *Surcouf*.

The aircraft hangar on the *Surcouf*. Above the hangar are two Hotchkiss 37mm cannon.

The two 203mm (8in) guns of the *Surcouf*.

A close up of the twin 8in guns of the *Surcouf*. (USN)

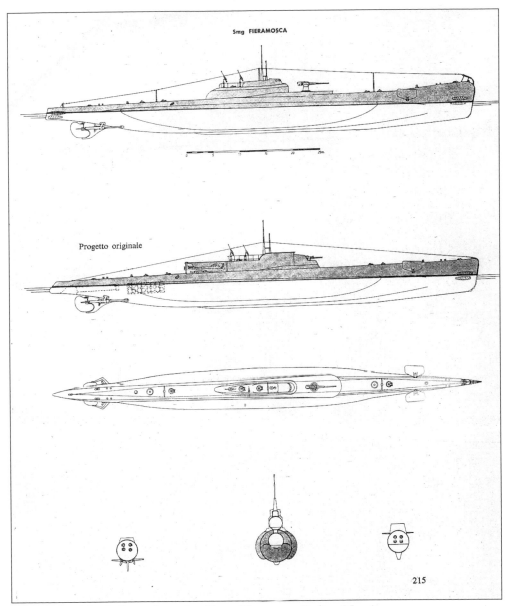

Drawings of the Italian submarine *Ettore Fieramosca*. (Italian Navy)

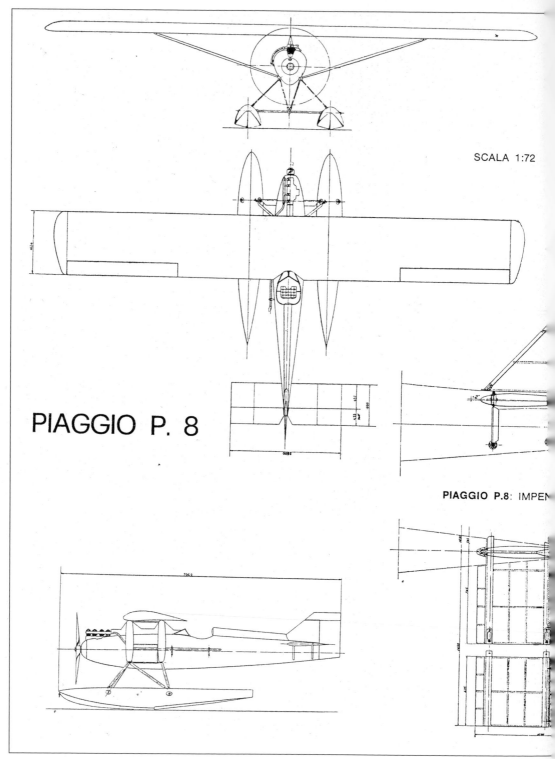

SCALA 1:72

PIAGGIO P. 8

PIAGGIO P.8: IMPEN

Drawings of the Piaggio P.8 aircraft that was designed to be carried by the submarine *Ettore*

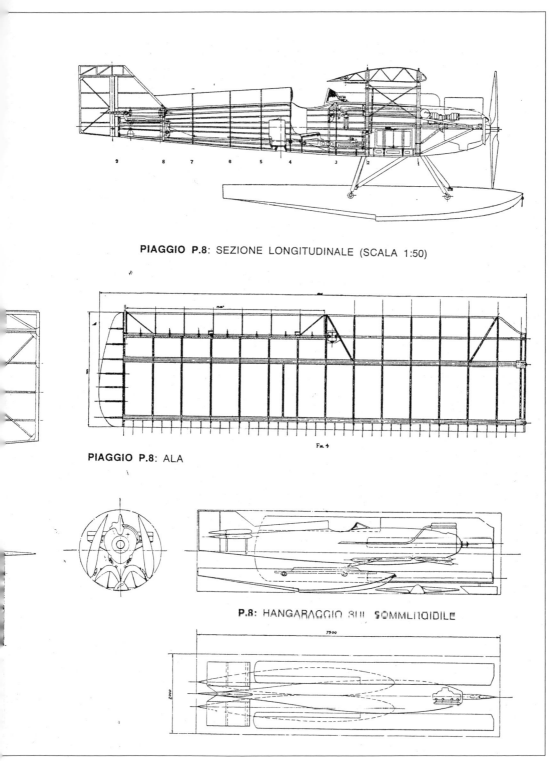

PIAGGIO P.8: SEZIONE LONGITUDINALE (SCALA 1:50)

PIAGGIO P.8: ALA

P.8: HANGARAGGIO SUL SOMMERGIDILE

Fieramosca. (Italian Navy)

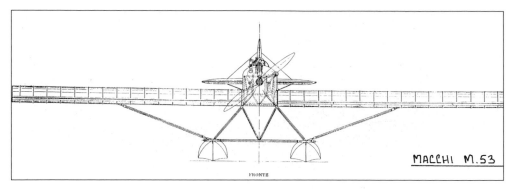

MACCHI M.53

FRONTE

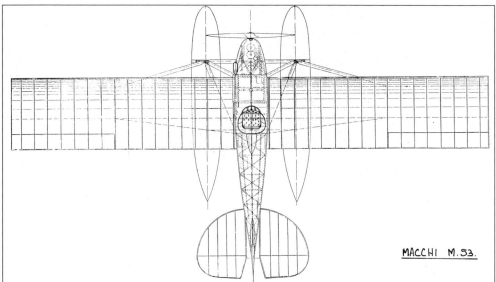

MACCHI M.53.

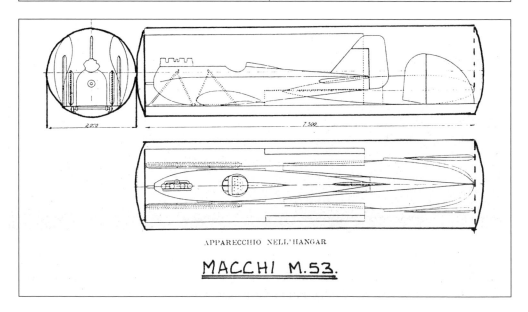

APPARECCHIO NELL'HANGAR

MACCHI M.53.

Side view of the Macchi M.53.

Above: Head-on view of the Piaggio P.8 being lifted from the water by crane.
Opposite: Drawings of the Macchi M.53. From top to bottom: a head-on view, a plan view and a diagram showing the configuration for hangar storage.

Loening XSL-1 experimental seaplane. Rear three-quarter view. (USN)

Loening XSL-2 – front three-quarter port side view on the ground.

A side view of a Japanese I-6 Class submarine. (USN)

The I-7 submarine with its full complement of crew on deck. (USN)

Overhead shot of the I-8. This submarine was equipped with the Watanabe E9W1.

Below: Close-up of an in flight shot of an early Yokosuka E14Y1 or 'Glen', as it was known to the allies, showing its two-man crew. (Bob Mikesh)

4 Necessity Becomes the Mother of Invention

With the advent of the Second World War the German Navy had also rekindled the idea of using submarine-borne aircraft and, in 1940, the Arado Flugzeug Werke was awarded a contract for six U-Bootsaugen or submarine eyes. They came up with the Arado AR 231, a high-wing, single-seat monoplane powered by an air-cooled, six-cylinder, inverted Hirth HN 501 160hp engine. The wings were designed in such a way that they folded one on top of the other atop the fuselage. The tiny aircraft fitted into a cylinder a little more than six feet in diameter. It was discovered during sea trials that the Ar 231 could not take off if the surface wind exceeded 20 knots. Again, as in 1917, the problem of rough seas prevented the use of a submarine-borne aircraft. For reasons best known only to themselves, the German Navy decided not to try and catapult the aircraft off the U-boats and, as the only other alternative was to lower the aircraft over the side by crane, it was decided that this was far too risky. In any event, the North Atlantic, on grounds of weather and sea state alone, would have been no place to operate small aircraft based on submarines so the idea was scrapped. However, as the German U-boat arm had been ordered to join forces with the Imperial Japanese Navy, there was a need to have larger, long-range submarines.

The IXD2 'Monsun' U-boat was the ideal boat to range further around the Cape of Good Hope into the Indian Ocean and on to Japan. A limited requirement could be foreseen for airborne observation posts that extended the U-boat's horizon in the broad oceans, where isolated targets of opportunity such as allied merchant ships might be found. From such requirements came the single-seat, and radically simple, Focke Achgelis Fa 330 Bachstelze (Water Wagtail) gyrocopter.

Although strictly speaking the Fa 330 was a rotary-winged kite, it was regarded as the smallest and without doubt the cheapest aircraft of the Second World War. Designed and built by the Focke-Achgelis Company, whose owner, Professor Henrich Focke, had been displaced as the chief designer of the Focke-Wulf Aircraft Company by the Nazis because he was deemed to be politically unsafe. He designed and built over 200 Fa 330s for use with the Kriegsmarine as an observation aircraft.

The Fa 330 had a three-bladed 24ft diameter rotor and weighed 180lb when assembled. The construction of the Fa 330 was very basic. The body consisted of an upright steel tube to which a rotor head was attached. A second longitudinal steel tube carried the seat, controls and instrument panel. Outrigger tubes supported short oval section steel tubes on each side. These served as skids when landing and taking off the submarine deck. There was a conventional tail unit consisting of a rudder, vertical fin and horizontal tail surfaces – there were no elevators. The

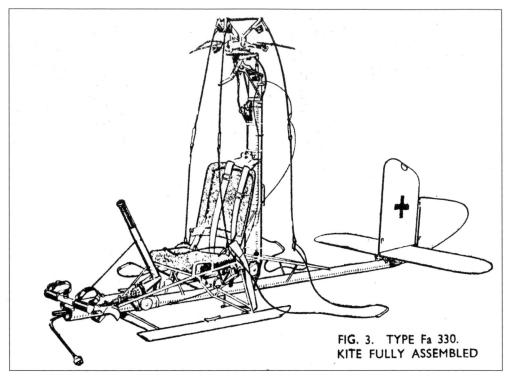

FIG. 3.   TYPE Fa 330.
KITE FULLY ASSEMBLED

Drawing of the Fa 330 rotorcopter.

method of assembling all the pieces together was very simple. There were only two points of attachment per unit; one was a wedge or pin fitting into a socket, the other a spring loaded pin that fitted into a female socket. The pins could then be freed by just squeezing them together. The whole thing was housed in two vertical, circular pressure-tight containers built into the deck. The containers were at the very least 12ft deep in order to accommodate all the parts. It was estimated that the entire gyrocopter could be assembled by four men in three minutes on a calm sea.

The aircraft, when assembled, was placed on a platform aft of the conning tower. The pilot/observer, who was normally a member of the crew, would strap himself into the seat and prepare for launching. The captain would then turn the submarine into the wind and increase the surface speed (a windspeed of 20 knots was required to get the gyrocopter airborne). The aircraft was then launched with a slight backward tilt of the rotor hub. The pilot's controls were of the conventional stick and rudder system. For the longitudinal system, pull-push rods and bellcranks were used throughout, but the lateral and rudder controls were operated by cables. The rotor blades were of the standard autogiro design and were untapered in plane and in thickness.

Operating speed was about 25mph, although the minimum speed to maintain flight was only 17mph. The normal operating height was between 200 and 500ft. Flown as a kite on the end of a steel cable, which also carried a telephone line enabling the pilot to communicate with the bridge, the Fa 330 was able to extend a U-boat commander's horizon from some twelve miles to a distance of perhaps fifty miles. This could be achieved in good visibility when the kite was flown at a height of 1000ft. When the mission was over, the aircraft was recovered by winding in the cable. Once on the deck, the rotor was stopped by means of a brake, allowing the blade hinges to be removed and the blades stowed away. The tail surfaces were then unlatched from the base and folded back against the main longitudinal tube and stowed. The outriggers were then folded laterally against the longitudinal member and that too was stowed.

The pilot/observer's position when aloft, was rather precarious in more ways than one. He would have to describe any vessel he saw with great care, because if he identified a warship, the submarine would more than likely crash-dive, leaving the pilot hovering and still attached to the submarine. In the event of this happening, the pilot would pull down on a lever attached to the rotor mast and this would jettison the rotor blades out of harm's way. As the rotor blades parted company with the rest of the aircraft, they would automatically pull a ripcord on the pilot's harness causing his parachute to open. When this happened, the pilot would then release his safety belt, leaving the rest of the gyrocopter to fall into the sea. This, in theory, would leave him to float gently down into the sea where, in the words of a Royal Navy report, 'he probably drowned in the normal way'. If he were lucky, he would be picked up by the submarine after the emergency was over. But the remains of what were later to be identified as Fa 330s were discovered floating in the Indian Ocean by the British, which leads one to wonder about the fate of the pilots.

The pilots were trained to fly the gyrocopters at the French Aeronautical Experimental Establishment at Chalais-Meudon, just outside Paris. The preliminary training was carried out inside a large wind tunnel and the advanced training was carried out by towing the gyrocopters, equipped with wheels, behind trucks along airfield runways. Experiments were later carried out by towing them behind a Fiesler Storch aircraft. There was also a proposal to convert the Fa 330 to a helicopter by fitting a 60hp engine, but the idea was shelved and eventually forgotten. By the end of the war, over 200 gyrocopter/kites had been built by the Weser Flugzeugwerke of Delmenhorst.

After the war, several of the Fa 330s were discovered at Laupien and were brought back to England for evaluation at Beaulieu House in the New Forest. They were found to be of an extremely clever, yet simple, design and were very well constructed. If one looks at the construction of these little gyrocopter/aircraft and compares them with the motorised gyrocopters of today, they are very similar. The German contribution to the use of submarine-borne aircraft was limited, although it is surprising that with the reputation of German ingenuity and engineering, they didn't make more use of the idea.

However, in 1943, a German Military Intelligence officer of Amt VI (the Central Office of Reich Security, a secret department of the SS), named Erich Gimpel, was given instructions to put together a plan to put the Panama Canal out of action. Called to Berlin by Sturmbannführer L., Deputy Head of the Department VIF, a section within Amt VI, Gimpel was told of Operation Pelican and the need to prevent the Allied ships using the Panama Canal. If closed, it would mean an 8,000 mile trip around the coast of South America to get from the Pacific to the Atlantic. This, of course, would slow down the huge American fleets and merchant ships as well as causing their fuel costs to spiral.

Gimpel listened carefully to the proposition and then asked how it was proposed to blow up the Panama Canal. The reply was short and abrupt. 'That is your affair. You can have anything you want to carry out the project – submarines, aircraft, men and what money you want. But it must succeed. From this moment you are in charge of Operation Pelican and you are responsible to me and no one else.'

For a moment Gimpel thought that the man was joking, then realised as he looked into pale blue eyes that the man had no sense of humour and that this department was answerable to the Führer himself. He was handed a letter authorising him to be afforded any assistance from all members of the military and that all of his demands be met without question.

As he left the room and stepped out into the sunshine, Gimpel reflected on his mission and on the piece of paper he had in his pocket. If this operation worked, it could alter the outcome of the war and, with the authority given to him with that simple scrap of paper, he was one of the most powerful men in Berlin, if not Germany, at that moment in time.

Erich Gimpel

Gimpel travelled to Breslau to meet the one person who knew more about the canal than anyone in Germany, an engineer by the name of Hubrich. Herr Hubrich had been one of the leading engineers on the Panama Canal when it was built and still retained a set of the original plans. Over lunch the two men talked about the operation. Although it was top secret, Gimpel knew that he had to take Hubrich into his confidence to enable him to get the necessary information. Gimpel's initial plan was to bomb the locks, but Hubrich quickly pointed out that they could be repaired in a matter of days. Herr Hubrich suggested that they go to his apartment and look at the plans. With the plans of the Panama Canal spread out on the floor, Hubrich pointed out that, to cause the greatest damage to the canal, the ideal place to bomb was the Gatun Dam which held back the Gatun Lake.

'In my estimation', said Hubrich, 'If the dam were to be blown up, the water would break through the dam, sweep over the canal and flow into the sea. The Panama Canal is built on a steep gradient, this was the difficulty in its constuction and once the dam is destroyed there would be nothing to prevent the water going back into the sea. I would estimate the damage would take at least two years to repair.'

Armed with this information Gimpel flew back to Berlin and straight to the Reich Air Ministry. At first he was greeted with the stony silence that most intelligence authors met with. Then he produced his special authority to a senior colonel and requested two Junkers Ju 87-C Stuka dive-bombers to be placed at his disposal. The request was granted.

Then, with a resigned voice – weighted with heavy sarcasm – the colonel asked Gimpel if he would be needing two volunteer pilots and ground crews to man the aircraft. 'Yes', was the short reply. Then, with a quizzical look on his face, the colonel asked how Gimpel proposed to get the aircraft and crews across the Atlantic. He received the curtest of replies, 'That's my affair!' Turning on his heel, Gimpel walked out of the office feeling extremely self-assured.

Next, Gimpel travelled to Keil to the Staff Headquarters of Grand Admiral Dönitz. Again he was greeted by a senior naval commander with the same distrust and resentment that he had received from the Luftwaffe. Once more he produced his authority, which was scrutinized by the commander, and was simply asked – what did he want? Gimpel asked for two Atlantic class V11C U-boats and their crews to be placed at his disposal for a period of ten weeks or so. This was at a time when the U-boat Wolfpacks were being stretched to their limits.

Gimpel then looked at the naval commander and asked if it was possible to get two dismantled Ju 87-C aircraft into the U-boats. 'Yes', came the reply, but accompanied by a rider that asked how he was going to reassemble them. Again, he replied as he had done to the air force colonel – 'That's my affair!'

He now had two VIIC class submarines and their respective crews, as well as two Junkers Ju 87-C Stuka dive-bombers, their pilots and mechanics. The two bombers had originally been designed for the ill-fated German aircraft carrier, the *Graf Zeppelin*. Gimpel then rented a long lakeside site on the Wannsee and turned it into a military area. There, an exact replica of the Panama Canal was constructed. The two

Front view of the Ju 87-C in folded configuration.

Stuka pilots carried out between ten and twenty dummy raids at varying heights each day as well as practicing landings and taking-off from the sandy soil of the foreshore.

The most difficult part of the training was of course the dismantling and reassembling of the two aircraft. After hours and hours of practice the ground crews managed to get it accomplished in two days. The U-boat crews also practiced stowing and removing the aircraft parts in the hull of the submarine. Four specially constructed high explosive bombs were then ordered and delivered to the site. Everything was ready!

On the face of it, the plan was relatively simple. The two submarines, with the aircraft aboard, would sail into the Caribbean sea, surface near a remote island and get the aircraft parts ashore. There, the aircraft would be reassembled and armed with the bombs. They would then take off and bomb the Gatun Dam. The pilots would then fly to a neutral country and land their aircraft. They would then have been interned for the duration of the war

In late September 1943 the crews were ready, the submarines were fuelled and provisioned for the long journey, and everyone had said their goodbyes to those on shore. As they prepared to get underway, Gimpel was informed that there was a telegram for him. Tearing it open he decoded the message:

Operation Pelican called off. Report to Berlin at once.

Gimpel was speechless and decoded it a second time in case he had made an error. But there was no mistake; all the hard work, energy and money that had been invested in the operation, had been for nothing.

On his return to Berlin, Gimpel was told that the whole operation had been exposed to the Americans and that the enemy would have been waiting for them. It would have meant the loss of not only two valuable submarines and crew, but also one of Germany's best agents. This was a risk not worth taking.

One aspect that was fortunately ignored by the German Reichsmarine, (fortunately for the Allies, that is) was the firing of rockets from submarines while they were submerged. At the beginning of 1942, Kapitänleutnant Fritz Steinhoff, commander of the U-511 brought his submarine to Swinemunde, which was near to the German secret missile base of Peenemunde. Fritz Steinhoff's brother was Dr Ernst Steinhoff, a rocket scientist based at Peenemunde. With the help of his brother, Fritz had managed to persuade his superiors to allow him to experiment with launching rockets from a submerged U-boat. A launching rack holding six conventional 'Granatwerfer' 42cm (16in) infantry rockets, were fitted on the port side just aft of the conning tower. Using wax to seal the exhaust vents and waterproof wiring laid inside the conning tower, the U-511 carried out tests off the Baltic island of Usedom. A number of tests were carried out, all successful, from varying depths down to seventy-five feet. With every launch the rockets ignited and, after they broke the surface, made successful firing runs. Why the experiments were not followed up is a mystery. One theory put forward was because of inter-service rivalry, but I find that very hard to believe considering the German position at that time. If they had taken up the experiments and improved on the rockets, who knows what damage they may have inflicted on the coastal cities of the United States and other Allied countries.

However, half a world away in the Pacific, the needs of the Japanese Navy for accurate information derived from reconnaissance, were to be rather more demanding. Now the rewards for Japanese persistence with submarine aviation were to become apparent. The new monoplane, reconnaissance floatplane, the Yokosuka E14Y1, codenamed the Glen by the allies, had been developed. This aircraft would perform reconnaissance tasks unimaginable a few years before, and would win a place in the annals of war. The first of the big Japanese submarines to have an aircraft hangar and catapult fitted to the front of the conning tower was the I-9. It had a length of 373ft and a beam of 31ft and carried one E14Y1 Glen. This, and later Japanese submarines, had a radius of action sufficient to undertake missions along the distant shorelines around the borders of the Pacific and Indian Oceans. In conjunction with a better performing aeroplane they constituted a formidable combination.

The first operational missions flown by E14Y1s involved reconnaissance flights from the submarine I-5 over Pearl Harbor in December 1941. The following month both the submarines I-9 and I-25 were equipped with aircraft. Encouraged by the success of these sorties, the I-25 moved into Australian waters where her E14Y1 made reconnaissance flights over Sydney Harbour on 18 February 1942, followed by a look at Melbourne on the 24th. Five days later the I-25 launched her aircraft again to make a successful flight over Hobart, Tasmania, radioing back shipping information to the submarine. On the evening of 29 May, an E14Y1 from

I-5 submarine on patrol in Tokyo harbour. This shot was taken before it was converted to become Japan's first aircraft-carrying submarine. (USN)

the I-21 made a reconnaissance flight over Sydney Harbour. The information gained resulted in four midget submarines attacking two American warships – unsuccessfully.

The I-25 and 26 left Yokosuka in May 1942, to carry out an air reconnaissance of Kodiak in the Aleutian archipelago. Submarine-borne air reconnaissance was becoming more and more hazardous and on two occasions both the I-26 and 25 had to crash-dive, only just managing to get their aircraft aboard and hangared. Later, off the Solomon Islands, the I-9 lost her aircraft when she had to crash-dive leaving her aircraft still on the deck. On 19 August, 1942, the I-17 was attacked on the surface while in the process of recovering her aircraft and was sunk.

In the Indian Ocean, the 4th Submarine Squadron was involved in a similar operational cruise. The aircraft-carrying submarines being the I-10 and the I-30. The E14Y1 from the I-10 made a reconnaissance of the harbour at Durban, South Africa, on 2 May and, a few days later, the harbour at Port Elizabeth. Meanwhile the I-30's aircraft flew reconnaissance sorties over Zanzibar, Aden and Djibouti, but none of those possible targets was considered to merit attack. The squadron then reformed and headed for Madagascar, where the Allies were landing at Diego-Suarez to take the island from the Vichy French. The I-10 launched her E14Y1 for a reconnaissance of the harbour. As a result two Japanese midget submarines were dispatched from their parent craft, entered the harbour, and sank an oil tanker as well as badly damaged the British battleship HMS *Ramilles*. Only one of the midget submarines returned and *Ramilles* had to limp to Durban for repairs.

In the meantime, the I-25 had joined the 1st Submarine Squadron on an operational cruise of the Aleutian Islands. Its purpose was to find locations for operational bases. However, but bad weather hampered the operations and only the I-25's seaplane was launched. Even so, the aircraft managed to locate an allied cruiser and two destroyers. The records don't say if they were subsequently attacked or not.

In March 1942, another attack on Pearl Harbor was planned – using long range flying boats and aircraft from submarines. The I-22 was assigned to prepare a refuelling base en route and set one up on an atoll named French Frigate Shoal. After carrying out preliminary reconnaissance between Hawaii and Midway Island she joined the I-15, I-19 and I-26 in preparation for the attack. The flying boats arrived from Jaluit and refuelled and the attack was carried out on March 5 on the island of Oahu. All the aircraft returned safely to the atoll. A second attack was ordered, but was cancelled when Wake Island was attacked by the Americans and the submarines were then deemed to be required elsewhere. It was fortunate for the Japanese that they did not return to the atoll, because their presence had been discovered and the area had been mined in their absence. A very unpleasant surprise would have awaited them if they had returned.

On 9 September 1942, an E14Y1 brought the war to the West Coast of the United States, when Lieutenant Commander Meiji Tagami, commander of the I-25 submarine, brought his boat to persiscope depth six miles off Cape Blanco, Oregon. He called Warrant Flying Officer Nobuo Fujita, Chief Flying Officer of the I-25, to the conning tower and invited him to look through the periscope. The sea was now flat calm after ten days of heavy weather and the pilot, who was about to make history, saw the white face of Cape Blanco and its lighthouse flashing in the twilight.

The I-26 scouting submarine on patrol. Its aircraft was housed in the hangar in front of the conning tower.

Japanese submarine I-15 on speed trials in Tokyo Bay. (USN)

Warrant Officer Nobuo Fujita turned to the captain and said 'Captain, it looks good. I think we can do it today.'

'Fine!' replied Captain Tagami. 'In a few more hours you will make history. You will be the first person ever to bomb the United States of America! If all goes well, Fujita, you will not be the last!'

The idea for the raid had come to Warrant Officer Fujita – one of the Imperial Japanese Navy's most experienced pilots with over 4,000 flying hours to his credit – while the I-25, together with the I-170, had been lying outside Pearl Harbor during the infamous attack of December 1941. Because his aircraft had been damaged by rough seas, Fujita could only sit and watch while the submarines I-25 and I-170 patrolled outside the harbour waiting to pick off any ships trying to escape.

On 10 December, they had reports that the aircraft-carrier USS *Enterprise* was steaming at full speed toward them and they were ordered to attack. Unfortunately for them, they were spotted by aircraft from the carrier and had to take evasive action, the hunters now becoming the hunted. Aircraft from the carrier dropped four bombs on the I-25, but Captain Tagami had managed to get his submarine well under the water and was lucky, but the I-170 was much slower and was sunk with the loss of all hands.

After this incident, Nobuo Fujita put forward the idea that if he were able to take-off from the I-25, he may be able to inflict substantial damage on the American ships. The I-25's Executive Officer, Lieutenant Tsukudo, was impressed by the suggestion and discussed in detail how he thought the Panama Canal Locks as well as aircraft factories and Naval bases around the San Diego and San Francisco areas, could be attacked.

In-flight shot of two Yokosuka E14Y1s.

'Put your ideas in writing to the Admirals in Tokyo,' said Tsukudo. Fujita laughed. 'Why would superior graduates who had studied at Etajima listen to a mere farm boy?' But at the insistence of Tsukudo he wrote a letter outlining his plans and gave it to the Executive Officer. In the months that followed, Fujita and his crewman Petty Officer Shoji Okuda, carried out a number of reconnaisance flights over Australia and New Zealand. These were hazardous flights because, had they been spotted by Allied fighters, they would most certainly been shot down. Because of this risk, Nobuo and Okuda agreed that they would lead the enemy aircraft away from the I-25 and crash the aircraft into the sea. If they survived the crash they would commit suicide.

The I-25 was involved briefly in the Battle of Midway and was off Vancouver when ordered to shell the US Naval base at Astoria, Oregon. After managing to get off seventeen rapid rounds of 5.5in shells the submarine set sail for Yokosuka on 9 July. Nobuo Fujita had forgotten all about the letter he had sent to the Japanese Imperial Naval Headquarters until, on 10 July 1942, Captain Tagami handed him a message:

> Warrant Officer Fujita is instructed to report to Imperial Naval
> Headquarters at once.

A nervous Warrant Officer Nobuo Fujita reported the following morning to the Japanese Imperial Naval Headquarters at Yokosuka. Entering the office of Commander Iura he was told that his idea had been accepted but he was going to bomb the American mainland and not warships. Minutes later the door opened and in walked another naval commander who Fujita immediately recognized as Prince Takamatsu, the Emperor's younger brother. Totally bowled over to be in such distinguished company, Warrant Officer Fujita could only vaguely remember what the meeting was about. He was shown a map of the West Coast and a point seventy-five miles north of the Californian border. He was to bomb the Oregon forests with two 76kg incendiary bombs. These bombs were of a specially powerful type which generated a temperature of around 1,500 degrees within a radius of 300 yards. At first Fujita was not too happy about bombing forests. He preferred to hit the cities of Seattle, Portland, Los Angeles and San Francisco, but he was told that the forests would burn, causing great devastation.

On the morning of 9 September 1942, Warrant Officer Nobuo Fujita and Petty Offficer Shoji Okuda made their final preparations by placing some strands of hair, fingernail cuttings and a will in a special box made of paulownia wood. In the event of the aircraft not returning from the mission, these remains would be sent to their families.

The E14Y1 Glen, piloted by Warrant Flying Officer Nobuo Fujita with his observer Petty Officer Shoji Okuda, was catapulted from the deck of the I-25 submarine and headed towards Cape Blanco lighthouse. After crossing the coast, the aircraft swung north-east for the forests of Oregon. After flying for about fifty miles, Fujita ordered Okuda to drop the first bomb, which burst in a brilliant white light, setting fire to the forest below. Flying east for a few more miles, he ordered the second bomb to be dropped, both bomb attacks causing fires. The aircraft then returned and rendezvoused with the submarine.

On the following day a second attack was made, again causing fires. On returning to the rendezvous point this time, Fujita discovered that the submarine was not in its pre-arranged position. After circling and searching, for what must have felt like an interminable time, he spotted some oil on the surface of the sea and by following it came upon the submarine. By sheer luck, coupled with an oil leak from the submarine, he had managed to find the proverbial needle in the haystack. The aircraft was quickly taken aboard and stowed in its hangar, but it had been spotted flying away from the forests by civilian observers, who notified the authorities. US aircraft were scrambled but sent in the wrong direction. A third raid was planned but the weather had turned rough so Lt Cmdr Tagami called it off.

Overall the damage caused by the bombing raids was minimal and the idea that it would cause great concern and possible panic to the American people never materialised. This was mainly because very few people ever knew of the attack until after the war, but the raids made history, being the only times the US mainland had ever come under aircraft attack. What would have been the result if Nobuo Fujita had had his way and attacked the cities we will never know. It may be speculated that had Nobuo Fujita had his way and cities had been attacked. the results might have been horrendous.

On the journey home, they received a message from Tokyo saying that

Portrait shot of Warrant Flying Officer Nobuo Fujita. Fujita has the distinction of being the only person to have ever bombed the United States of America.

according to a radio broadcast in San Francisco, 'an aircraft, presumably from a submarine, had dropped incendiaries on the Oregon forest area causing some casualties and some damage.' The sea was being scoured for the I-25 by both aircraft and ships so Captain Tagami kept the submarine submerged all day, only surfacing after dark to recharge her batteries. The I-25 continued her patrol and during the first half of October sank two oil tankers off the west coast. With her last torpedo she sank a US submarine before returning to home waters. On his return to Yokosuka, Nobuo Fujita was hailed as a hero, his theory of carrying out bombing raids from submarines a proven fact. He was to see out the war as a flying instructor.

The only other recorded time that the American mainland was attacked during the Second World War was in November 1943 and March 1944. The Imperial Japanese Army Special Balloon Regiment launched 9,300 thirty-five feet diameter hydrogen-filled paper balloons from East Honshu, Japan, to drift with the prevailing winds the 6,000 miles across the Pacific. Many of the balloons were found between Alaska and Mexico. The exact number is not known. The balloons were armed with two small incendiary devices and a 35lb anti-personnel bomb. The only known casualties were a woman and five children, who unwisely picked one up. It is interesting to note that this happened in Oregon, as did the first attack

Japanese balloon bomb that carried high explosives. They were launched from Japan and landed in Mexico, the USA, Canada and Alaska. This one was found intact in Canada.

in 1942. The successful use by the Japanese of submarine-launched aircraft for reconnaissance and attack purposes in 1942 had amply proved the concept.

A growing list of operational requirements – uninterrupted zeal, suitable parent craft and crews dedicated to making the system effective under the impetus of war – all combined to make Japan's submarine aviation more effective that any other nation's up until the end of the Second World War. From 43 degrees south, and from 32 degrees east to 124 degrees west, strategic harbours could be reconnoitred by an aircraft with a range of no more than 550 miles. The I-11 was fitted out as a squadron flagship and carried extra communication facilities. In 1942, changes were made to the submarine, in which the double-acting, two-cycle engines were changed to single-acting, solid injection four-cycle engines. Although this reduced the power from 12,400-shp to 4,700-shp, the engines were smaller and weighed less, consequently the fuel capacity was increased by thirty-seven tons and the cruising radius increased to 22,000 miles at sixteen knots.

The overrunning of many islands in the Pacific, which were strategic specks in the ocean, was to create more problems for Japan than solutions. Islands require garrisons which need to be supplied. As the United States built up its naval strength both on the oceans and above it, re-supply became progressively more difficult. Japan had foreseen the problem to some extent and had begun to lay down a fleet of very big submarines to operate re-supply missions to her island bases.

Meanwhile in Japan, the navy was progressing on its latest weapon; a weapon so secret that the allies did not find out about it until after the Japanese had surrendered. The weapon was a giant submarine, that was best described as an undersea aircraft-carrier and given the classification of the I-400 Class. The design of the giant submarines started early in 1942. Eighteen were planned and the construction of four of them began in February 1943, the first one being completed late in 1944. Only the I-400 and I-401 were ever finished, the remaining two, the I-403 and I-404 were never completed and were destroyed during construction by American bombers.

The Sen-Toku (Submarine Special) boats of the I-400 Class were 400ft long and

The hangar of the Japanese submarine I-400 which housed three 'Jake' type aircraft. This submarine was 400ft long and 40ft wide and displaced over 3,000 tons. (US Navy)

had a maximum beam of 40ft. They had a displacement of 3,900 short tons on the surface and were capable of cruising for 37,500 miles without refuelling. Incorporated into the 400ft hull and in front of the conning tower, was a 120ft hangar set amidships and capable of carrying three aircraft. Because the I-400 Class submarine could linger on the surface longer than an ordinary submarine, extra consideration was given to protection from machine-gun fire, by the use of extra thick metal plating in the construction of the conning tower and hangar. Her armament consisted of eight bow tubes and twenty torpedoes, as well as normal deck guns.

Building these leviathans required so much time, and cost so much money as well as labour and materials, that the project was discontinued after the first two were completed. As a replacement the I-13 Class submarines were to be modified to take two aircraft, the only problem being that the submarine had a smaller radius of action. Of the four designated to be converted, only two were completed before the end of the war.

During the construction of the I-400 Class submarines, the long range B-25 bombers of Jimmy Doolittle's raiders had attacked the Japanese mainland. This caused the Japanese to think of ways of retaliating but they realised neither their aircraft or ships could get near enough to the American mainland without detection. It was decided that the only way to attack was with submarine-borne special attack aircraft. The Imperial Japanese Navy approached the company that had made aircraft exclusively for them throughout the war – the Aichi Aircraft Company. Their president, Kamatoro Aoki, and their chief designer, Norio Ozaki, had already been having secret talks with the navy about such an aircraft

The Aichi M6A1 Sieran land model.

and the Doolittle raids on Japan served only to speed them up.

On 15 May 1942, the Kaigun-Koku-Hombu (Naval Aviation Headquarters) gave the Aichi Company the specifications for the aircraft that was to be called the Experimental 17 Shi-special Attack Bomber. Now the term 'Special Attack' was invariably associated with Kamikaze aircraft, such as the navy's Ohka (Cherry Blossom) rocket-propelled suicide aircraft, which could only be described as a bomb with wings. It was the intention of the navy to use the Experimental 17 Shi-special attack aircraft for the following purpose; this aircraft was to be the first purpose-built; submarine-based aircraft that had a strike mission as its primary role. Although the design of the aircraft was similar to that of the carrier-based dive bomber, the Yokosuka D14Y1 Suisei, it became necessary to redesign it so that it would fit into an 11ft 6in-diameter hangar on a submarine. There was a six-inch clearance at the tip of each propeller when the aircraft was inside the hangar and this did not leave a lot of room for mis-handling. The name given to this aircraft was the M6A1 Navy Special Attack Bomber Sieran (Mountain Haze).

The engine selection was both critical and limited. Three different engines were considered, the Mitsubishi Mk.8 of 1,300hp, the Nakajima NK 9B Homare of 1,800hp and the Aichi Atsuta 32 of 1,400hp. The first two were radial cooled engines and considered the most reliable, but their relative sizes caused a problem. Because of the limited space between the bottom of the fuselage and the hangar deck it was impossible to hang a torpedo or bomb from the fuselage. Unfortunately, it was necessary to have the armament in place when the aircraft was stowed. Also to be taken into consideration was that when the submarine surfaced to launch its aircraft the submarine was at its most vulnerable and time was of the essence. It was therefore much safer to arm the aircraft while it was in its hangar and the submarine submerged.

The Aichi Company made a full scale mock-up of the aircraft out of wood which enabled them to work out any problems with the intricate design. The main design feature that had to be perfected, was the folding back of the wings against the fuselage. The method devised by Aichi had the wings pivoting on the main spar where it joined the fuselage, then by rotating it downwards the wing could lay flat against the fuselage, much like the Grumman Avenger. The top part of the rudder folded down to give it hangar clearance and the two pontoon floats were removed and housed in their own container below the level of the deck. When launching, the whole of the aircraft was lowered almost to track level, by collapsible, compressed air-activated struts on the heavy catapult car. The cockpit was designed for a crew of two who were housed in a veritable greenhouse giving them all round visibility. The armament carried, besides the bombs or torpedoes, was a 13mm Type 2 machine gun mounted in the rear cockpit. With the detachable floats, folding wings and tail surfaces, it was estimated that four fully trained men could prepare the Sieran for launch in under seven minutes.

Now it would be possible to specify aircraft performance more comparable with conventional carrier-borne attack bombers. The greed of military dictatorships has a habit of outstripping the resources available to the and so it was with Japan's truly

Japanese submarines I-14, I-401 and 400 at Guam after the Japanese surrender. Each of these submarines could take three Sieran aircraft in the hangar on the deck.

formidable combination of Aichi M6A1 aircraft and the I-400 Class submarines. With all the trials of this potentially formidable combination completed, a plan was drawn up by the Imperial Japanese Navy to attack the Gatun Locks of the Panama Canal. If the attack was successful, the raid would create havoc with the moving of men and supplies into the Pacific theatre of the war. The plan was to launch ten of the Sierans from the I-400 Class submarines, attack the lock gates, return to the submarines and crash-land alongside them, pick up the crews and submerge. This would leave the enemy wondering where the attack came from and whether or not they would strike again.

The whole force was put under the command of Captain Tatsunoke Ariizumi who, through his persistence, persuaded the Japanese High Command to abandon their plans for an attack on the US mainland and attack the Gatun Locks instead. He argued that a successful attack on the Panama Canal lock gates would cause more damage to key equipment and to morale that any attack on the US mainland.

Training for the raids on the Panama Canal did not progress well. The crews practised their bombing runs on a large scale model of the Gatun Locks, but were constantly being interrupted by attacks from aircraft from US aircraft-carriers. The beginning of July 1945 brought the first submarine flotilla together, which consisted of the I-400, I-401, I-13 and the I-14. The task force was equipped with ten aircraft. The two smaller submarines, the I-13 and the I-14, did not have the fuel capacity for the round trip to the Panama Canal and were to be refuelled from the bigger boats. Using the same route that was used by the Pearl

The Aichi M6A1 Sieran floatplane on its beaching trolley.

The Japanese fleet at anchor after the surrender. In the foreground are their giant aircraft-carrying submarines. (USN)

Harbor attack force the four submarines, provisioned for a four-month cruise, set sail for Oahu. It was intended that they would head southwards down towards the Colombian coast, then the submarine force would alter course and move in a northerly direction hugging the coastline. When they were in range of the locks, the submarines would surface and launch their Sieran aircraft. Each aircraft would carry either a torpedo or a 1,764lb bomb. After take-off the pilots would jettison their floats so as to increase their diving speed when they attacked.

But time ran out for the flotilla, instead of the attack on the Gatun Locks, they were diverted to attack the Ulithi Atoll, where US aircraft-carriers were anchored. On 16 July, about 630 miles east of Honshu, the I-13, commanded by Commander Chashi, was spotted and attacked by a submarine-hunter group from the USS *Anzio* (CVE-57). Although badly damaged by rockets, the I-13 managed to give them the slip, only to be tracked down and sunk by the destroyer USS *Lawrence C. Taylor*.

The remaining boats did not press home their attack but altered course to rendezvous off Ponape Island in the Eastern Carolines and they were still there when hostilities ended. Not one of the giant submarines ever saw action in spite of all the time, money and manpower spent on them. Ordered to return to Japan, the giant submarines made their way to the Yokosuka Naval Base, where Captain Ariizumi committed *hara-kiri* in atonement for the disgrace of having surrendered. The captured submarines, after they had been subjected to detailed scrutiny by the US Navy, were used as targets for naval gunfire practice and were sunk. Only one of the Aichi M6A1 Sieran seaplanes survived and is now on display at the National Air and Space Museum in Washington.

The Aichi M6A1 Sieran floatplane discovered virtually intact in a bombed-out hangar after the war and now on display in Washington. (USN)

The German Arado Ar 231 V1 collapsible floatplane in assembled form.

The Ar 231 V1 floatplane stowed inside its container.

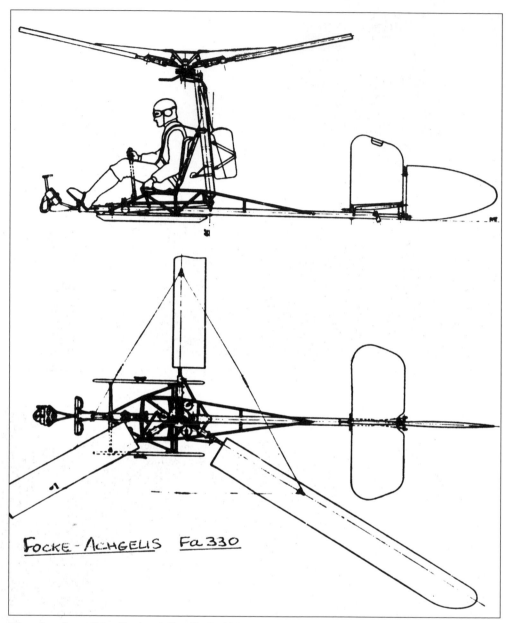

Plan drawing of the Focke-Achgelis Fa 330 rotorcopter.

German U-boat crew members removing the rotorcopter from its waterproof deck canister.

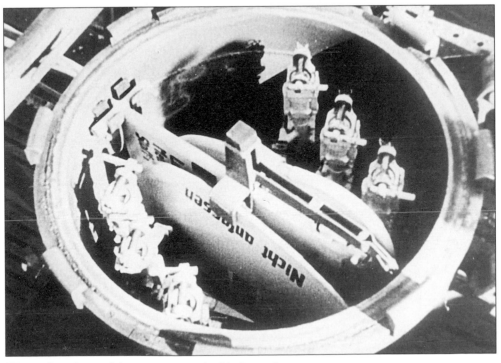

View of sections of the rotorcopter inside its canister.

German submariners removing the tail section of the rotorcopter from the canister. The winch and rope are visible.

The main seating section being removed from the canister

Tail section being assembled on the deck.

Rotors being fitted to the rotorcopter.

Assembled rotorcopter on its launching platform behind the conning tower.

Preparing the rotorcopter for launch.

Close-up of the pilot in the rotorcopter just clearing the launch platform but still being held by the launch crew.

The rotorcopter just taking off from the submarine.

A view of the conning tower and the rotorcopter becoming airborne.

Shot of the rotorcopter at about fifty feet. Its operational ceiling was about 1,000ft.

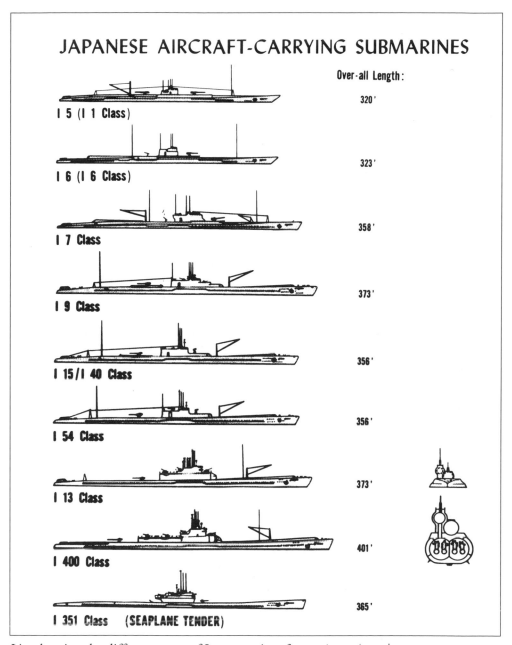

JAPANESE AIRCRAFT-CARRYING SUBMARINES

Over-all Length:

I 5 (I I Class) — 320'

I 6 (I 6 Class) — 323'

I 7 Class — 358'

I 9 Class — 373'

I 15/I 40 Class — 356'

I 54 Class — 356'

I 13 Class — 373'

I 400 Class — 401'

I 351 Class   (SEAPLANE TENDER) — 365'

List showing the different types of Japanese aircraft-carrying submarines.

I-16 submarine on patrol.

I-17 Class submarine during its commissioning ceremony.

I-54 submarine on trials. (USN)

A Yokosuka E14Y1 being prepared for launch from an I-Class submarine. The recovery crane is already extended. This photograph must have been taken in 1942 as only the deck and hangar top have been painted black and the *Hinomaru* flag is still laced to the side of the conning tower.

Yokosuka E14Y1 climbing away after being catapulted from the I-29 submarine. This aircraft could be assembled ready for flight in ten minutes by only seven men.

Yokosuka E14Y1 about to be launched from an I-400 Class submarine. A view taken from the bridge of the submarine. The marks are water stains on the photograph.
Previous pages: A Yokosuka E14Y1 on its beaching trolley. (Bob Mikesh)

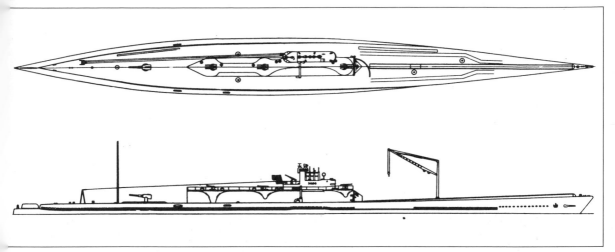

Outboard profile and deck plan of the I-400 Class submarine.

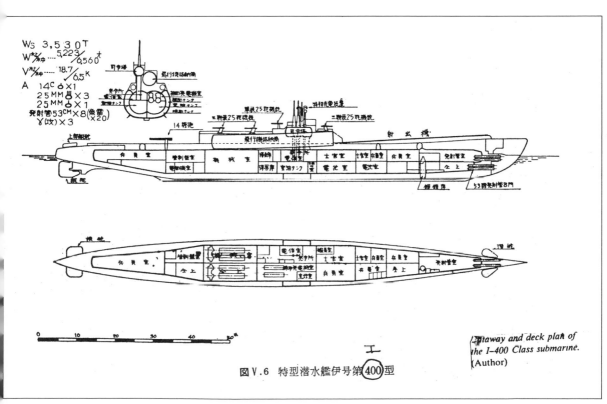

図V.6　特型潜水艦伊号第400型

Cutaway and deck plan of the I-400 Class submarine. (Author)

Cutaway and deck plan of the I-400 Class.

An excellent view of the launching rails on the I-400 submarine. Note the retracted crane on the port side. (USN)

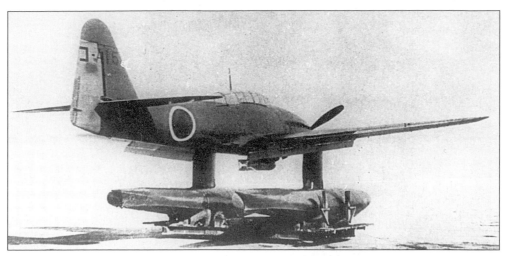

A rear three-quarter view of the Aichi M6A1 Sieran floatplane on the slipway. (USN)

Storage tubes for aircraft floats aboard the Japanese submarine I-400 on the starboard side of the main aircraft hangar.

The I-14, I-401 & I-400 at Guam, November 1945. This shot was taken from the submarine tender USS Proteus (AS-19) as crews unloaded stores from the captured submarines. It also shows the enormous size of the Japanese submarines. (USN)

The Japanese submarines I-400, I-401 and I-14 alongside the American submarine tender USS *Proteus* (AS-19) at Yokosuka on 7 September 1945. All three submarines have their collapsible aircraft cranes in the raised position. In the background can be seen the Japanese battleship *Nagato*, which survived the war only to be used as a target during the Bikini Atoll atomic bomb tests in July 1946.

Stores being unloaded from the I-400 class submarines. (USN)

The I-14, manned by a US Navy crew, being brought alongside the I-401 at Guam in 1945. (USN)

The I-14 and I-400 moored alongside the Submarine Tender USS *Proteus*. (US Coast Guard.)

Officers of the I-401 submarine after their surrender. (USN)

Japanese captain of the Submarine I-400, Commander Toshiwo Kusaka listening intently to an interpreter during interogation.

The I-402 at Guam. (USN)

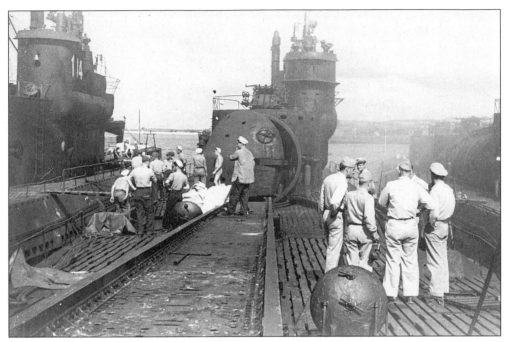

Japanese submarines I-14, I-401 & I-400 at Guam, November 1945, while en route from Japan to Pearl Harbor. This shot taken aboard the I-401. Each of these submarines could take three Sieran aircraft inside the hangar on the deck. (USN)

Japanese submarines I-14, I-401 & I-400 at Guam, November 1945. This view shows the tremendous size of theses vessels. The aircraft-launching ramp is clearly visible. (USN)

The Japanese aircraft-carrying submarines I-400, I-401 and I-14 at Pearl Harbor after the war (bottom right-hand corner).

5   The French Connection

Of the main Western combatants in 1939, Germany, Britain and France, only France had submarine-based aircraft in service – one example was on the *Surcouf*. Submarine aviation was not to be the Western way and for good reasons. As Britain received her supplies across the North Atlantic, the German U-boats attacked Allied ships at the choke points and along convoy routes. Many of these vessels were 517 and 720 ton ships known as Liberty Ships that had been built quickly and in quantity. When France fell to the Nazi hordes storming across Europe, the *Surcouf* sailed from Brest to Plymouth, England, to join the Free French Navy. Relations between the French and the British, never good at the best of times, were becoming strained and uneasy and an unexpected visit to the submarine by Vice-Admiral Dunbar-Naismith, Commander-in-Chief Devonport and Lt Patrick Griffiths from the submarine HMS *Rorqual* did nothing to enhance the relationship.

Three days earlier *Surcouf* had been moved from her berth, to be moored alongside the French battleship *Paris*. It hadn't escaped the notice of the respective crews that not only would it be difficult to sail without the British knowing, but that the 15in guns of the British battleship HMS *Revenge* were now pointed directly at both ships.

On 3 July 1940 at 0415 hours, *Surcouf* received a coded message from Admiral Darlan's headquarters in France, saying that the British were about to attack the French fleet at Mers-el-Kébir, Oran, Algeria and that *Surcouf* was to be scuttled. A few days earlier, Darlan had given Winston Churchill his assurance that the French Fleet would never fall in to German hands. Then Marshal Philippe Pétain offered Darlan the position of Minister of Marine in the Vichy regime, which he readily accepted. He reiterated his promise to Churchill but the British Prime Minister would not trust him because the Vichy regime operated in France in co-operation with the Axis powers. As a result, Churchill ordered an attack on the French Fleet. The signal to *Surcouf* arrived almost at the same time as word came from the conning tower that the British were boarding the boat. The French crew on watch had been watching the gang plank and the quayside and had not seen a boarding party of five officers and twenty-eight ratings from the submarine HMS *Thames*, together with a party of Royal Marines from HMS *Revenge*, approaching from the seaward side. A series of tragic events then occurred aboard *Surcouf*, resulting in the deaths of three British sailors and one French sailor. Not since the Battle of Trafalgar in 1805 had the French and the British navies fought each other in hand-to-hand combat.

With over 75% of the original crew interned, *Surcouf* was made ready for sea with as motley a crew as could be assembled in such a short period of time. They consisted of Breton fishermen, merchant navy seamen and even farmers,

The French submarine *Surcouf* tied up in Plymouth harbour.

most of whom had never seen a submarine let alone served on one. On 20 December 1940, *Surcouf*, under the command of Commander Ortoli, set sail with a three-man British naval liaison team aboard. The team, arranged by Admiral Horton, consisted of an officer and two telegraphists, who were responsible for all communications, ciphers and recognition signals and also ensured that all Admiralty orders were fully understood by the French captain.

The trip was a type of 'shakedown' cruise for both the submarine and its crew, but the resentment of the British by the French crew smouldered beneath the surface for the whole trip and the inexperience of the crew did not help. After returning to Plymouth for the Christmas and New Year, *Surcouf* was ordered to set sail for HMS *Titania* (the submarine supply ship) in the Clyde area for training in attack and night operations. Two weeks later Admiral Horton, after receiving reports on the problems that *Surcouf* was experiencing both as a submarine and with its crew, ordered *Surcouf* to set sail for Halifax, Nova Scotia, where it was hoped it could be put to some use as a convoy escort. After a long and arduous voyage that took twelve days to complete, *Surcouf* arrived in Halifax. It was decided that after repairs the submarine would at first undertake a series of trials, followed by operational cruises.

The operational cruises were a disaster from day one and *Surcouf* was ordered back to Plymouth. Admiral Horton had found that the problems involved with the submersible leviathan and a French crew that bordered on the incompetent, were insurmountable. On arrival back in Plymouth, the little MB-411, which had been on board in its hangar for the duration, was taken off for minor repairs and servicing. While ashore, the already long-lived little aircraft was damaged beyond repair in a German bombing raid and this effectively put paid to *Surcouf*'s aircraft carrying career. The pilot, Sergeant Jacques Hazard of the French Air Force, now without an aircraft, was transferred to No.10 Squadron of the RAAF, flying Sunderland flying boats on anti-submarine patrols.

After a great deal of thought, Admiral Horton decided that because of *Surcouf*'s diving problems, he would send her to the South Atlantic to hunt for German merchant ships. The reasoning behind this was that there was virtually no air patrols in this part of the world and *Surcouf* could operate in relative safety from the surface. She was to operate from Bermuda as an independent command. Although this may sound as if *Surcouf* was something rather special, in reality no one knew what to do with a giant submarine that had major operational problems and a crew to match.

During the voyage to Bermuda, *Surcouf* had suffered a series of electrical fires and desperately needed major repairs. When it was realised that the repairs could only be carried out by a fully-equipped naval repair yard, the Admiralty in London signalled the British Advisory Repair Mission in Washington to arrange for *Surcouf* to be repaired at the US Navy Yard in Portsmouth, New Hampshire. On 25 July *Surcouf* was ordered to Portsmouth, New Hampshire, for refitting and repair work in Dry Dock No.2, arriving there on 28 July. As big as *Surcouf* was, she was lost in this enormous facility that, at the time, was handling repairs to three British submarines, HMS *Truant*, *Pandora* and *Parthian*, together with over fifty American submarines either under construction or in for repairs. The cost of the repairs and refitting work to *Surcouf*, was estimated to be at around $800,000, all to be paid under the Anglo-American Lend-Lease Programme.

Problems started to manifest themselves almost immediately. Because of the

The submarine *Surcouf* at Halifax, Nova Scotia, in 1941.

disgusting state of the *Surcouf* both inside and out, the dockyard workers insisted on bonus payments before they would even start work on the giant submarine. There were no plans or drawings available to the dockyard and this meant they would have to produce their own, creating even more problems because all technical terms on the equipment were in French. Weeks turned into months as the problems continued to mount, and it was the end of October before the *Surcouf* was ready to return to Bermuda to continue her role.

After carrying out a series of sea trials off New London, Connecticut, in which *Surcouf* was involved in a collision with an American submarine, she was ordered back to Bermuda. But instead of heading south, the *Surcouf* headed north towards Halifax, Nova Scotia. It appears that Commandant Blaison, who was now in command of the submarine, had been ordered there so that Vice-Admiral Muselier could inspect all the units of the Free French Navy that were operating in the area. During her time in the Halifax area, *Surcouf* was involved with the capture of a small group of islands off the coast of Newfoundland. They were St Pierre and Miquelon and were governed by Gilbert de Bournat, a Vichy sympathiser. Strategically placed at the mouth of the St Lawrence River, it was believed that the large powerful transmitter on St Pierre was sending back vital information to the Vichy government in France.

Surcouf left St Pierre on 11 January 1942 for minor repairs in Halifax. After these had been completed, she left for Bermuda on 3 February, arriving on the

The damaged bows of the American freighter SS *Thompson Lykes* after allegedly colliding with the French submarine *Surcouf*.

7th. Just after she had left, secret orders were received saying that it was unsafe to call at Bermuda, followed almost immediately by a message from Admiral Horton, ordering the boat to operate out of Tahiti and go to there via the Panama Canal.

On 12 February 1942, *Surcouf* left the Bermuda area for Colon, via Caicos, the Windward Passages and the Panama Canal. On 18 February 18 an American steamship, SS *Thompson Lykes*, under time charter to the US Army, sailed from Cristobal on a voyage to Guantanamo Bay, Cuba. The ship was a single-screw cargo vessel, about 417ft long with a 60ft beam, weighing 6,763 tons gross and 4,016 tons net. At around 2230 hours the same day and travelling at about 13 knots, a bright white light was spotted off the starboard bow. The lights immediately went out. The junior third mate ordered the rudder hard left, but before the ship could respond the light appeared again, this time directly ahead and close to the bow of SS *Thompson Lykes*. This indicated to the crew on the bridge that the unknown vessel was passing across the bows, starboard to port. The rudder was ordered hard right in an attempt to pass under the stern of the other vessel but almost immediately the bow of SS *Thompson Lykes*, collided heavily with the unknown vessel. No trace of the vessel or any survivors were ever found.

The report on the collision reads as follows:

April 3,1942.
Secret and Confidential

Rear Admiral R.R. Waesche,
Commandant, US Coast Guard,
Washington, D.C.

Re: S/S Thompson Lykes - February 18, 1942
Collision with Unidentified Vessel

Sir:

Pursuant to the provisions of Title 46, U.S.C. 239, as amended, and your letter of appointment dated March 9, 1942, the undersigned "A" Marine Investigation Board convened at New Orleans, La., on March 11, 1942, to conduct an investigation into the circumstances attending the reported collision between the American Steamship Thompson Lykes and an unidentified vessel, which occurred in the Caribbean Sea on the night of February 18, 1942, about eighty (80) miles North-Northeast of Cristobal breakwater.

During the course of the investigation, the Board examined eleven (11) witnesses, all members of the crew of the Thompson Lykes, including the master, chief engineer, third assistant engineer, junior third mate, two able seamen, an ordinary seamen, oiler, fireman, and two United States Army privates; and, according to the testimony of these witnesses, the collision occurred under the following circumstances:

On the afternoon of February 18, 1942, the American Steamship *Thompson Lykes*, a single screw steel cargo vessel, about 417.9 feet long, 60.0 feet beam, 6,762 gross and 4,016 net tons register, owned by Lykes Brothers Steamship Company and under time-charter to the United States Army, sailed from Cristobal, C.Z., on a voyage to Guantanamo Bay, Cuba, "for orders". The *Thompson Lykes* was partially loaded with Army cargo, her draft on sailing being about 10'6" forward and 16'8" aft, or slightly more than half her normal full loaded draft of about 28'2".

Prior to sailing from Cristobal, the master of the *Thompson Lykes* had conferred with and obtained written sailing orders from the US Navy, as to operation. Copies of these sailing orders were not available to the Board, because they had been returned to the military authorities at Cristobal when the *Thompson Lykes* returned to that port after the collision, but the master testified that the sailing orders merely directed him to proceed to Guantanamo Bay "for orders", under total blackout conditions. The orders did not prescribe any specific course or speed, nor did they contain any information with respect to other vessels which might be encountered en route. Accordingly, he assumed that he was authorized to take the normal trade route from Cristobal to Guantanamo Bay.

After leaving her berth at Pier 6, Cristobal, the *Thompson Lykes* proceeded down the harbor to a point just outside the breakwater, and dropped her pilot. At 4:40 P.M., E.S.T. (75th meridian) the *Thompson Lykes* took 'departure' for Navasea Island on a course of 27 by gyro, to make 28° true, at her full speed of about fifteen knots. At the time of departure the weather was overcast, with good visibility, and a moderate sea.

The *Thompson Lykes* proceeded in this manner until about 6.30 p.m., when, because of a heavy swell, she reduced speed to approximately thirteen knots. In accordance with her sailing orders, all navigation lights were extinguished and the vessel was totally dark. At 8:00 p.m. the master decided to proceed direct to Guantanamo Bay, instead of via Navasea island, and he changed course from 28° true to 23° true.

At 9.45 p.m., pursuant to a coded message received from the Canal Zone to proceed to Cienfuegos, rather than Guantanamo Bay, the master made a further change of course from 23° true to 356°.

Having made the last mentioned change of course, the master left the bridge and went into his office, leaving written orders to be called in the event of an emergency. Thereafter, navigation was in charge of the junior third mate (a master mariner with some thirty years experience) who was on the bridge with the able seaman at the wheel. An ordinary seaman was stationed on lookout, in the crow's nest with another able seaman on standby duty. In addition, there were two Army privates on deck duty as members of the ship's gun crew. One of the privates was on lookout on the flying bridge, while the other was on lookout near the stern. Both were instructed to keep a sharp lookout and report any lights or other objects to the bridge.

At about 10.30 p.m., while proceeding on the aforesaid course of 360° true, at about 13 knots, the junior third mate, the helmsman, the lookout and the Army private on the flying bridge suddenly observed a small, bright, white light, about a point on the starboard bow of the *Thompson Lykes* a short distance away. Each of the witnesses described the light as one such as would be shown by an ordinary hand flashlight, the beam of which was directed toward the bridge of the *Thompson Lykes*. The light was extinguished immediately after it was observed, but in order to give clearance to the unknown vessel from which it had been shown, the junior third mate ordered the rudder hard left. However, before the Thompson Lykes could answer her rudder, the light appeared again directly ahead and close to the bow of the Thompson Lykes, indicating that the other vessel was crossing the course of the Thompson Lykes from starboard to port. Accordingly, the junior mate ordered the rudder hard right, in an attempt to pass under the stern of the other vessel, but almost instantly the bow of the Thompson Lykes collided heavily with the other vessel.

Prior to the collision those on board the Thompson Lykes did not see the hull of the other vessel and the only warning of her approach was the above described light. No whistle signals were sounded by either vessel before or after the collision.

The force of the collision retarded the speed of the Thompson Lykes momentarily, and then a brilliant sheet of flame shot up from the water on both bows of the ship. The witnesses described this sheet of flame as similar to an oil explosion and said that, shortly afterwards, they could smell the odour of burning oil. The sheet of flame disappeared immediately and a few seconds later the loom of the other vessel, lying low on the water, was observed passing down the port side of the Thompson Lykes. When it was about abreast of No.3 hatch, forward of the bridge, it was observed disappearing under the surface of the water. In the darkness it was impossible to observe even the shape of the sinking vessel, although one witness described it as being similar to the bow of a submarine. Immediately after the unidentified vessel sank, a violent underwater explosion shook the Thompson Lykes and another sheet of flame arose from the surface of the water.

Immediately before or immediately after the second explosion the voices of one or two men were heard calling for help. The Army private on lookout near the stern testified that he saw and heard a man in the water, wearing what appeared to be a white 'sweat-shirt', calling for help as he passed astern. However, the voice disappeared in the darkness and from that moment no trace was ever found of any survivors.

As soon as he felt and heard the collision, the master of the Thompson Lykes ran out on the bridge and immediately stopped the engines. He then manoeuvred his ship around and returned to the place of collision. With the aid of the ship's searchlight, a diligent search was made for survivors and wreckage, but the only evidence of a collision was a large patch of oil on the surface of the sea, part of which was known to be coming from the double-bottom tanks of the Thompson Lykes.

The Thompson Lykes remained in the vicinity of the collision until about 7.15 a.m. the following morning when she got under way and proceeded to Cristobal for survey and temporary repairs.

According to an observation obtained before leaving the scene of the accident, the collision occurred in about Lat. 10° 40' North, Long. 79° 31' West, approximately eighty miles North-Northeast of Cristobal breakwater. The time of the collision was estimated to be 10.30 p.m., E.S.T.

Conclusions

The Board, having seen and heard the witnesses, is satisfied that the collision was purely accidental and, so far as the personnel of the Thompson Lykes was concerned, unavoidable.

When the single white light was first shown by the approaching vessel, off the starboard bow of the Thompson Lykes, the vessels were already 'in extremis' and collision could not have been avoided by any action on the part of the Thompson Lykes. The junior third mate attempted to avoid collision by directing his course to port, but when the light re-appeared dead ahead, the order was countermanded and the course was directed to starboard. It is probable, however, that the net effect of these two orders was to leave the Thompson Lykes on her original course of 356° true at the time of the collision.

While the engines of the Thompson Lykes were not stopped or reversed until after the collision, there is nothing to indicate that the collision would have been avoided, or the damage mitigated, if such an order had been given before collision. The interval of time was so short that the collision probably would have occurred before the engineer on watch had time to operate the throttle.

The Board also concludes that although the lookout was stationed in the crow's nest, about 150 feet from the bows, instead of 'at or near the bow' (General Rules & Regulations, Rule V, Section 25 as amended), this did not contribute to the collision. The night was dark, but visibility was good, and the white light was apparently sighted by those in charge of the Thompson Lykes at the instant it was shown by the approaching vessel.

The Board concludes, therefore, that the collision was not due to ant fault or neglect on the part of the Thompson Lykes, or those in charge of her, but that it was caused by the operation of the two vessels intersecting courses, without lights due to the exigencies of war.

Unfortunately, the testimony failed to disclose the identity of the lost vessel and, since there were no survivors, the Board is obliged to conclude that the Thompson Lykes collided with an unidentified vessel, of unknown nationality, resulting in the total loss of the vessel and her crew. Although the witnesses were convinced that they rammed an enemy submarine, there is nothing in the evidence to support that conclusion.

The Board therefore recommends that the investigation be closed without further action.

Respectfully

———————————, *Chairman*

Harold B. Finn, Esq.
Special Assistant to
the Attorney General.

———————————, *Member* ———————————, *Member*

Captain J.L. Ahern,   *Mr. John F. Oettl.*
United States Coast Guard   *U.S. Supervising Inspector.*

There have been numerous theories on what happened to *Surcouf*; some say that it was deliberately sunk by the British, others that it was accidentally bombed by the American Army Air Corps. All that is known is that she disappeared and that her last calculated position put her approximately where the collision with

SS *Thompson Lykes* took place. James Rushbridger's book *Who Sank the Surcouf* goes into great detail about the disappearance of the *Surcouf*, but this is where I intend to leave it.

One story that circulated after the war was that the British had planted limpet mines on the *Surcouf*, and if the giant submarine headed for the Panama Canal as she had been ordered, then they would tell the French so that they could remove them. But if, on the other hand, they headed for a more questionable port the British would remain silent and let the mines run their course. The story says that the *Surcouf* did just that and headed for the island of Martinique, which was strongly suspected of giving help to U-boats because of the Vichy influence that governed the island. The mines are said to have exploded and sank the *Surcouf* with all hands – or so the story goes.

Officers of the *Surcouf* in the wardroom. From left to right: François Boyer; Louis Blaison (captain); Georges Russignol; André Leoquet (gunnery officer) and Pierre le Grand (second engineer).

Following pages: General de Gaulle leaving the French submarine *Surcouf* after visiting it while it was in Plymouth harbour.

The crew of the *Surcouf* going below after the visit of General de Gaulle.

The submarine *Surcouf* undergoing trials in the Holy Loch, Scotland, sometime in 1940.

Starboard three-quarter view of the *Surcouf* in dry dock No.2 for repairs at Portsmouth Navy Yard, New Hampshire, USA.
Following pages: Bow shot of the *Surcouf* while in dry dock in New Hampshire. (USN)

Rear three-quarter view of the *Surcouf* in dry dock. (USN)

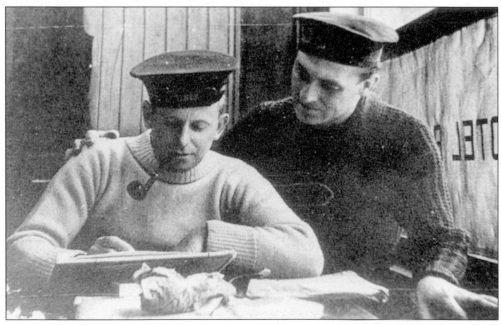

The two British signalmen on the *Surcouf*. On the left is Leading Signalman Harold Warner and on the right, Leading Telegraphist Bernard Gough. Both these men perished in the *Surcouf* when she disappeared.

6   The Development Years

During the closing stages of the Second World War, Germany had launched both unmanned pulse-jet aircraft (V-1) and ballistic rockets (V-2) against Great Britain from their secret rocket base at Peenemunde in the Baltic. There was even a proposal to launch V-2 rockets from large containers towed by U-boats. The launching platform was to be a huge float fitted out with fuel tanks and launching gear. When the towed float reached its destination offshore, the ballast tanks at the rear of the float would be flooded so the launching platform and rocket would stand vertically. Technicians would then fuel the rocket and prepare it for firing. The launch itself would be activated from the submarine. A number of trials were conducted and although relatively successful, development difficulties and the instability of the rocket itself caused the project to be cancelled. The demise of the German rocket base sealed the fate of these rockets.

From that moment, an inevitable great divide opens up between the various military authorities and scientists when considering submarine aviation. From 1945, when manned aircraft could still be envisaged as operating from, or in conjunction, with submarines the future lay principally with unmanned vehicles.

The sudden end to the Second World War found the United States in possession of over 1000 'Loons' that had been copied from the German Fiesler Fi 103 (V-1). The JB-2 'Loon' was an exact copy of the Fiesler Fi 103 or Vergeltungswaffe Eins (Revenge Weapon One) as the Germans knew it, or V-1 'Doodlebug' or 'Buzz Bomb', as the British came to know it.

Between June and September 1944, an average of 180 Doodlebugs per day were launched against England. Originally the Fi 103 was a manned vehicle and was developed under the code name of *Reichenberg*. The test pilots were Flugkapitan Hanna Reitsch – an internationally famous woman test pilot – Hauptmann Heinrich Lange and SS-Hauptsturmführer Otto Skorzeny. Initially the idea was that pilots and their fighters would be launched from beneath the port wing of Heinkel He 111 bombers. The pilot would then aim his fighter at a pre-selected target and then bale out. After a great deal of experimenting it was decided that the pilots had less than a hundred to one chance of surviving, so the Fi 103 was re-designed as an unmanned vehicle.

The JB-2 developed by the Americans was the result of obtaining a crashed Fi 103 that had not exploded. The wreckage was flown from England to Wright Field and in only seventeen days American technicians had produced an exact copy of the V-1's Argus-Schmidt 109-014 pulse jet engine, utilising both American and German parts. By the end of six months the technicians and scientists from the Ford and Republic

JB-2 `Loon' ready for launch on its rocket-propelled sled. (USN)

Companies had their own copy of the V-1 ready for testing. The Monsanto Chemical Company then produced the solid rocket fuel boosters and the whole programme was moved to the Mojave Desert for the start of test launches at Muroc Dry Lake (later Edwards Air Force Base). The first tests of the 'Loon' had been carried out late in 1944, when a JB-2 was launched from Range 64, Eglin Field, Florida, over the Gulf of Mexico.

The War Department decided to carry out tests with a number of copies of the Fi 103 and authorised an expenditure of $90 million to this end. The trials were called Project MX-544. Extensive research was carried out with these ground launches but with very limited success. It was to take over fifty test launches before the problems were overcome. Serious consideration was then given to launching the JB-2 Loon against Japan. As if to endorse this proposal a number of air launches were carried out from converted B-17 bombers. Out of ten launches carried out in the spring of 1945 at Wendover, Utah, from B-17s, only four were successful. Later the B-17 was replaced with the B-29, but it made no difference to the results so the use of aircraft to launch the JB-2 was dropped. It was decided to use them as expendable test vehicles in the nuclear cruise missile programme.

Thoughts then turned to alternative ways to launch the missile. In 1946, US Navy Secretary James Forrestal approved the conversion of two BAOLO Class submarines into guided-missile launchers. The submarines that were to be converted were the USS *Carbonero* (SS337) and the USS *Cusk* (SS348) and the weapon they were to launch was the 'Loon'. The 'Loon' was later to provide crucial information and experience in the cruise missile programme. The first of the submarines to be converted was the USS *Cusk*. The conversion consisted of the installation of a rocket-type launching ramp, a topside watertight hangar that would house the Loon and a launching sled with rockets.

On shore the tests had been carried out using a short ramp and a rocket-assisted launcher. The tests were so successful that in January 1947 a ramp was fitted to the aft deck of USS *Cusk* but problems with the installation of the missile itself caused a delay. The installation of the ramp on the aft deck entailed the removal of the aft

JB-2 `Loon' launching from the deck of the submarine USS *Cusk*. (USN)

gun. It was also pointed out at this time that if the missile hangar were flooded the submarine could not submerge safely as the volume of the hanger was greater than the volume of the safety tank. When all these problems had been resolved, the only thing that prevented the first launch taking place was that the Lockheed P-80 chase aircraft was not ready.

On 18 February 1947, Commander P.E. Summers, USN, positioned the USS *Cusk* one and half miles from Point Mugu, California, in preparation for the first launch of the Loon from a submarine. The sea was calm and the wind was blowing a steady eight knots. At 14.41 hours, the Loon was launched. The missile and sled blasted off the deck of the submarine in a cloud of smoke. The sled dropped away into the sea immediately on leaving the deck but, unfortunately, the missile did not stabilise and crashed into the sea some 600 yards away. As was usual with all these kind of tests, a camera recorded the whole launch and flight. It was noted when viewed later that, when the rockets burned out, the missile, although in a satisfactory position for the flight, did not stabilise the moment it left the sled. The nose lifted, one wing appeared to dip and then it climbed away at a very steep angle until its engines burned out and it subsequently crashed.

There were a number of trials after this and the majority of them were successful, including one in which the missile, after an apparently successful launch and flight, refused to respond to the signal to dump into the water. The accompanying P-80 aircraft that was escorting the missile, in case situations like this arose, was ordered to shoot it down. The pilot attacked the missile but ran out of ammunition without effecting any damage on it. Fortunately for him, the Loon responded to a pre-set launch command and dived into the sea, much to the relief of everyone.

The C-in-C, Submarine Forces, US Pacific Fleet, regarded all tests to be successful and gave orders for the USS *Carbonero* to be assigned to the Loon project, with the 'Gorgon IIC' surface-to-surface missiles. At the same time plans were underway to replace both these missile programmes with the 'Regulus' missile programme.

To represent both lines of thought, the work done by the US Navy with the Chance Vought Regulus I missile has to be mentioned. Starting in 1951 this command-guided, surface-to-surface, bombardment missile (to give it its title at this period) underwent tests starting on 29 March 1951 from the seaplane tender USS *Norton Sound*. Powered by an Allison J33-A-14 turbojet of 4,600lb thrust, assisted by two Aerojet solid-rocket boosters, the initial trials required an unobstructed landing area. This was followed by a second launching on 3 November 1952 from the aircraft carrier CV-37 USS *Princeton*.

In 1952 Ed Heinemann, noted chief engineer and designer at the El Segundo Division of Douglas Aircraft, had, at the Navy's request, designed a small attack aircraft capable of being stored on the deck of a ship. Called the Douglas Attack Aircraft Model 640, it was 32ft 11in long, had a wingspan of 25ft unfolded – 9ft 3in folded – and was 10ft 4in in height. It was capable of being stored inside a Regulus hangar. This JATO-assisted turbojet aircraft, with a fuselage designed to act as a hull on touchdown before recovery, did not receive the go-ahead. Later technology was to catch up with it on the development front.

Between February 1952 and March 1953, the submarine USS *Tunny*, after conversion, was used to launch two Regulus I missiles. A second submarine, USS *Barbero,* was converted to carry the Regulus I and a number of tests were carried out. The first Regulus I looked more like an aircraft than a missile and two diesel attack

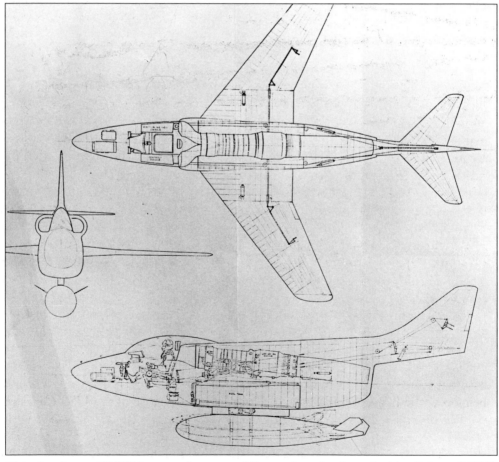

Plan drawings of Ed Heinemann's proposal for a submarine-launched jet fighter. (USN)

Rare shot of the Regulus I missile in flight with its undercarriage down and with an accompanying chase aircraft. (USN)

submarines, USS *Growler* and *Grayback*, were converted to become her launching pads. Fitted with retractable landing gear, the Regulus started its flight trials on 29 May 1955. Before the end of the year, the Regulus I was reaching speeds of more than Mach 1.5 at heights of 50,000ft. As with the Loon project, the Regulus I was accompanied for safety reasons by a Lockheed P-80 aircraft, in the event of a guidance malfunction. The idea was not a new one – during the Second World War, Spitfires of the Royal Air Force had flown alongside German V-1 rockets in an attempt to turn them around or make them crash by using their wingtips to upset the gyroscopic navigation system of the V-1.

The nuclear-powered submarine USS *Halibut* was chosen to be fitted out to carry five Regulus I and two Regulus II missiles but, although some launches of the Regulus I were carried out, the programme was cancelled before the refit was completed.

The first launching of a Regulus II missile from a submarine was on 16 September 1955, when the USS *Grayback* launched the missile while in the Pacific. The launch was a complete success.

The problems that had surrounded the shipbuilders when they built or converted submarines to carry aircraft or missiles, had been vast, the obvious one being that the hangar would have to watertight. In the case of the USS *Carbonero*, she was originally designed as a conventional submarine. This meant that the hull had to be split amidships, the fore and aft sections moved apart, and a new 50ft section inserted. This new section was required to provide space for the launching rails and hangar. The hull had to be redesigned from the bow to a point 70ft aft,

Aerial shot of the USS *Grayback* at her commissioning ceremony, showing the two missile hangars on her bows. (USN)

so that the 11ft-high hangars could be built into the forward section. This meant that the forward torpedo tube doors had to be welded shut. After redesigning, the construction continued normally and she was completed and launched on 5th April 1958.

Firing the missile was a well-rehearsed procedure. As soon as the submarine surfaced, one of the faired hangar doors was opened, giving access to the inner hatch of the hangar. The missile was then winched out backwards on a rotatable launcher. The wings were then unfolded and locked into position. When the launching cables had been secured, control surfaces checked out and the safety wires pulled from the JATO (Jet Assisted Take-Off) bottles, then the missile was ready for launching. When fired, the roar emitted from the winged missile made conversation impossible within the submarine. After the first launch, the only damage that could be found on the exterior of the submarine, was blistered paint.

In 1957 a number of surface ships, among them the heavy cruisers *Helana, Los Angeles, Macon and Toledo*, were fitted out with facilities to launch both the Regulus I and II missiles. The submarines had proved their usefulness and were being prepared for another stage in the development of missiles being launched from submarines.

In the same year, Lockheed's Missile and Space Company began work on a solid propellant, two-stage missile to be fired from a submarine while underwater. Within little more than a decade, more than forty-one submarines of the US Navy were in commission, each carrying sixteen Polaris A2 or A3 missiles, following an industrial and development programme that was unprecedented in its scope and urgency during peacetime.

This line of development has, of course, continued since in the Soviet Union (now the CIS), United States, Britain and France. The German initiative in 1915 to put a fragile reconnaissance seaplane on the deck of a submarine has escalated to unbelievable heights in just over half a century and with a vengeance.

Is there a place on board the submarines of tomorrow for another manned aircraft when missiles can strike at long range or intercept close-in with devastating accuracy? With military satellites for surveillance and navigation satellites for position fixing, the role of the manned aircraft carried in a submarine would appear to be limited. Bearing in mind the finance likely to be required to produce a workable system for what appears to be limited objectives, the chances for the utilisation of the manned airplane appear to be slim.

There is however, a potential candidate in the shape of the VTOL Harrier or its successors should an operational requirement ever arise. To widen the potential acceptability of the Harrier in the world's smaller navies, British Aerospace conducted studies to determine whether its unique-vectored thrust VTOL aircraft could be operated from ships in the 200 to 300 ton class.

Deck motion, even in a modest sea state, was shown to be unacceptable. With the naval helicopter, decades of experiment and trials had overcome the problem,

Experiment in the use of helicopters on submarines. (USN)

Skyhook being tested using a crane and a Harrier. The aircraft is being flown by the Skyhook's innovator, Heinz Frick, Harrier test pilot.

the helicopter being constrained immediately on touchdown by equipment incorporated within the deck.

For the Harrier, the BAe solution was to eliminate the undercarriage and make the aircraft operable from a trolley, in association with a gyroscopically stabilised crane. This crane, known as 'Skyhook', would retrieve the aircraft from the hover position alongside the ship and play a similar role when dispatching a Harrier sortie.

On the approach, sensors locate the Harrier, which is captured in hovering flight by directing a probe jack to the aircraft pick-up point, located on top of the fuselage behind the cockpit. Once locked on, the aircraft is pulled up and firmly docked onto pads. The Skyhook is then swung inboard, the head of the crane becoming increasingly ship-stabilized, thus allowing the aircraft to be placed accurately on the ship's deck. The initial concept was proved on land, at Dunsfold, Surrey, in 1983 when a Harrier, piloted by company chief test pilot Heinz Frick, made a series of tests with a converted mobile crane.

It is but several practical steps away to imagine this pioneering concept being applied to an aircraft-carrying submarine. An outlandish idea? Possibly, but not one that can be dismissed lightly on the grounds of technical feasibility as the known problems have shown themselves to be amenable to solution.

Submarines are already in service of a size comparable to the light anti-submarine aircraft-carriers of the Royal Navy's Invincible Class (19,500 tons). For example, the US Navy's Ohio Class SSBN (Fleet Ballistic Missile Submarine - Nuclear) submarines (16,600 tons) and the Russian Typhoon Class SSBN submarines, reputed to be in excess of 30,000 tons, are more than capable of operating operational VTOL aircraft. Skyhook is a revolutionary and radical concept.

If the Skyhook concept were ever to gain acceptance, the term 'attack submarine' could take on a whole new meaning.

Regulus I missile ready for launch aboard the USS *Tunny* (SSG-302) off Point Mgu on 26 August 1954. (USN)

The Regulus I missile aboard the USS *Grayback* (SSG-574), entering San Diego Harbour. (USN)

Previous pages: The Regulus I missile being launched from its pad at Point Mugu, California. Note the chase aircraft in the background. (USN)

Above: Regulus I missile being fired from the submarine USS *Halibut*, with the aircraft carrier USS *Lexington* in the background. (USN)

Regulus missile with its JATO bottles just ignited, launching from the deck of the aircraft carrier, the USS *Hancock*. (USN)

Regulus I missile being readied for launching aboard the submarine USS *Barberro*.
Previous pages: USS Cusk (SS 348) being fitted out with a Regulus hangar.

Regulus II missile being launched at Point Mgu, California. (USN)

Regulus II missile being launched from the submarine USS *Grayback*. (USN)

USS *Grayback* entering San Francisco harbour.

Regulus missile ready for launch aboard submarine USS *Grayback*.

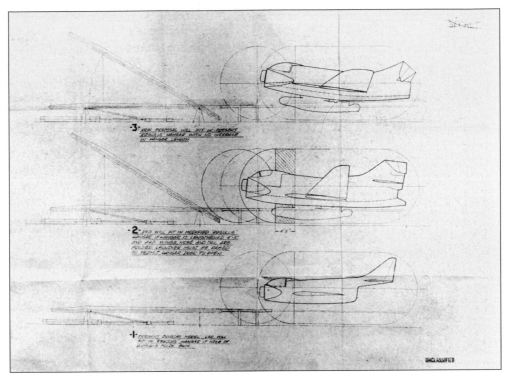

Drawing of three Douglas designs for aircraft that would fit in the Regulus hangar. The lowest is the Douglas Model 640. (USN)

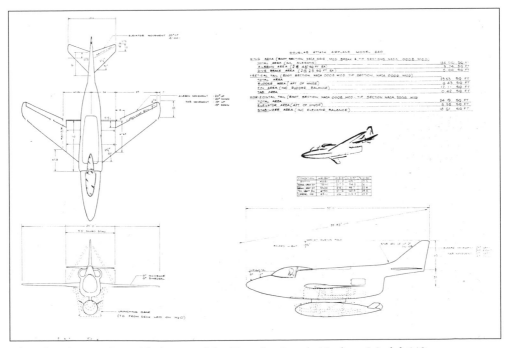

Plan drawings and specifications of the Douglas Attack Airplane Model 640.

Above: A model showing the launch and recovery system for an aircraft by Grumman. The aircraft, called the Nutcracker, was swung out onto a loading platform to be launched. After launch it was recovered in the same manner. (Grumman)

Shot of the Nutcracker model in the hover position.

Martin P5M-1 Marlin, using a submarine (SS362) as a tender. (USN)

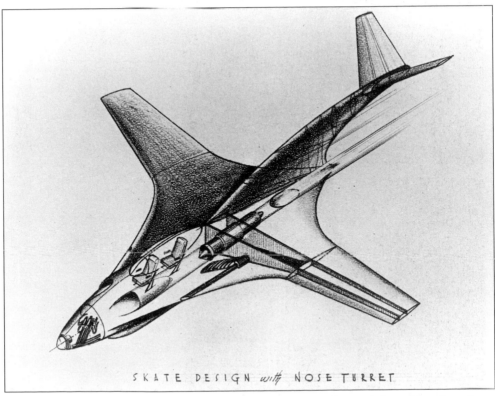

Drawing of the Convair Skate aircraft, which was designed to be used alongside submarines.

A one-tenth model Skate alongside a one-tenth model submarine in 1952.

Another view of the model Skate aircraft and submarine.

Postscript

The most difficult aspect of combining submarines and aircraft is not the design and engineering but the acceptance of a radical idea by the scientific and military staffs and, ultimately, the government offices. This book clearly illustrates that the engineering skills of fifty years ago were perfectly adequate to achieve a major and tactical breakthrough. The fact that submersible aircraft carriers have not been fully developed since the Second World War merely underlines the fact that both naval and air staffs are most reluctant to divert from the well-trodden guide lines and military manuals.

Defence chiefs appear to be content to spend increasing sums of money on defence equipment that is sometimes largely compromised by politics. Inter-service rivalry and party politics appear continually to dilute the quality and quantity of our defensive equipment. It is incredible that some foreign navies, for instance, are not allowed to operate fixed-wing aircraft because that is regarded as the job of the air force and the air force, in turn, is not prepared to go to sea.

One wonders how many good ideas have never matured from the drawing board because of the 'not invented here' syndrome and the 'don't confuse me with facts, my mind is made up' attitude. It is particularly in the field of warfare where technical innovation can win the day. No one doubts the virtue of flexibility, surprise, mobility and stealth and no better way are they demonstrated than in the submarine and the VTOL fighter.

The most obvious way of achieving fixed-wing aviation from a submarine in the future is by way of VTOL aircraft as typified by the Harrier and the recently developed Skyhook system. The Harrier, even after its success in the Falklands and the Gulf conflicts, is still the most misunderstood fighter in the world. Its tremendous power and agility in combat, its persistence because of its low fuel consumption and its ability to land virtually anywhere make it a formidable weapon. The fact that it can operate from carriers and dispersed grass airfields has only been fully appreciated and accepted by Britain, the US Marine Corps and the Spanish Navy.

Conventional fighter aircraft that require thousands of yards for take-off still sell in large numbers. Such large airfields are of course difficult to defend and the cost of the overall operation is further increased by the necessary acquisition of guns, missiles, concrete hangars etc.

Airfields do not move, cannot be hidden and cannot be defended effectively against a co-ordinated attack by ground and air forces. That is a fact, although an airfield of course does have one advantage – it cannot be sunk. The large aircraft carriers are indeed airfields that have the advantage of mobility, but suffer from limited operational usefulness when at the bottom of the ocean. The modern argument is that the carrier and its aircraft are there to protect the fleet and the fleet is there to protect the carrier. Nobody really wins. In peacetime the cost of the overall operation is crippling and in wartime the sinking of one aircraft carrier is catastrophic. The owners of these ships point out that no aircraft carrier has been sunk since the Second World War, forgetting the fact that no major war has occurred since then and that a certain amount of luck was enjoyed in the Falklands and Gulf conflicts. The fact that the Harrier does not necessarily have to operate from large carriers gives it a unique advantage at sea which could, of course, be further enhanced if the ship were submersible.

Submarines are not new and neither are the tactical advantages offered by moving silently below the surface. A submarine that is capable of accommodating aircraft is clearly not going to be small. The problem is not overwhelming when one compares the Ohio Class SSBN, or the even larger Russian Typhoon Class SSBN of 16,000 tons, with HMS *Invincible*, a through-deck carrier of 19,500 tons.

A submersible aircraft carrier would not necessarily require the same depth performance as current submarines. If one assumes that such a vessel can be built and that the Harrier type of aircraft is suitable, that is going some way into producing a modern submarine with wings. But any idea that so fundamentally changes established, well proven lines of development must take time to find acceptance and support. The frustrating aspect for designers is that it akes too long.

Index